Also by the Author

BPMN Method and Style (2nd edition 2011)

BPMN Quick and Easy (2017)

DMN Cookbook (2018)

DMN Method and Style
2ND Edition
Business Practitioner's Guide to Decision Modeling

Bruce Silver

DMN Method and Style 2nd Edition, Business Practitioner's Guide to Decision Modeling

By Bruce Silver
ISBN 978-0-9823681-7-6

Published by Cody-Cassidy Press, Altadena, CA 91001 USA
Contact
        info@cody-cassidy.com
        +1 (831) 331-6341

Library of Congress Subject Headings
Industrial management--Decision making--Mathematical models
Information visualization
Process control -- Data processing -- Management.
Business -- Data processing -- Management.
Management information systems.
Agile software development.

Cover design by Leyba Associates

TABLE OF CONTENTS

Log into the Trisotech DMN Modeler and click File/New. Drag out a decision and label it *Loan Approval*. Drag out input data elements *Credit Score* and *DTI*, and then click the yellow triangles to connect the information requirements as shown in Figure 17.

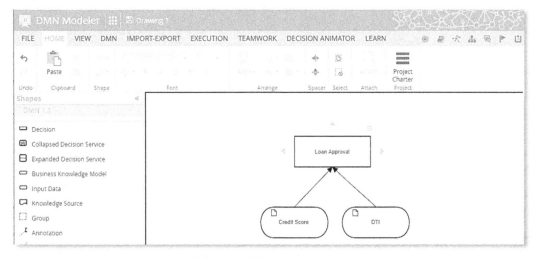

Figure 17. DRD in Trisotech Decision Modeler

Now define the datatypes. *Loan Approval* is text with enumerated values "Approved" and "Declined". *Credit Score* is a number from 300 to 850 inclusive. *DTI*, which stands for debt-to-income ratio, is any number. We can define the types either in the DRD or in the decision table for *Loan Approval*. Here it's easier to use the decision table, so right-click the decision, Attributes/Decision Logic and select Decision Table. If you've connected the information requirements, the table column headings should be filled in already, but with the default type Text.

In the *Loan Approval* column, click on the default type Text, define constraints of type Enumeration, and enter values Approved and Declined. Then click the button *Create Type*, which will create an item definition for you, default name *tLoanApproval*, with those enumerated values (Figure 18).

Type:	Text	
Constraints:	Enumeration	▼
Values:	"Approved"	✏ ✕
	"Declined"	✏ ✕
		☑

Create Type   Close

Figure 18. Custom type with enumerated values

Now in the *Credit Score* column, click on Text and change it to Number, click on Number and add constraints, type Simple, min 300, max 850, and change the parentheses to square brackets. Parenthesis in a numeric range means exclude the endpoint; bracket means include it. Again click Create Type to create the item definition (Figure 19).

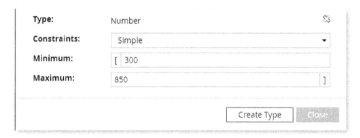

Figure 19. Custom type with defined range of allowed values

In the *DTI* column just change Text to Number. Here we have no constraints, so we don't need an item definition.

Now your table heading should look like this:

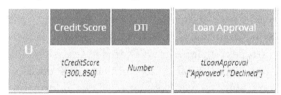

Figure 20. Type and allowed values shown in decision table column headings

Here are the rules for Loan Approval.

The value is "Declined" if:

1. *Credit Score* <600. Since *DTI* is irrelevant in this rule, its input entry is hyphen.

2. *Credit Score* is between 600 and 660 inclusive and *DTI* >=0.35. A numeric range input entry separates the minimum and maximum values with two dots and uses bracket to include the endpoint, parenthesis to exclude it.

3. *Credit Score* >660 and *DTI* >=0.38.

The value is "Approved" if:

4. *Credit Score* is between 600 and 660 inclusive and *DTI* <0.35.

5. *Credit Score* >660 and *DTI* <0.38.

Swap the position of rules 3 and 4 by dragging them in the tool, grouping by *Credit Score* condition. Now on the Home ribbon, select the *Credit Score* column and click *Merge Similar Cells*. The result should look like Figure 21.

	Credit Score	DTI	Loan Approval
U	tCreditScore [300..850]	Number	tLoanApproval ["Approved", "Declined"]
1	<600	-	"Declined"
2	[600..660]	>=0.35	"Declined"
3		<0.35	"Approved"
4	>660	>=0.38	"Declined"
5		<0.38	"Approved"

Figure 21. Decision table with merged cells

Merging adjacent cells is optional in DMN decision tables. Some believe it makes the tables easier to read.

On the DMN ribbon, click *Method and Style Decision Table Analysis*. This tool feature checks the table for completeness, consistency, and other style errors. It should show no errors (Figure 22). Save your model.

Log Viewer

Severity	Message
ⓘ	Method and Style Validation completed without errors on 1 table.

Figure 22. Decision Table Analysis shows no errors

To see how Decision Table Analysis works, let's create some errors. Change the left bracket in the *Credit Score* input entry for the merged rule 2/3 to left parenthesis, and in rule 5 change the *DTI* input entry to <=0.38. Now when you run Decision Table Analysis you should get something like Figure 23, indicating a number of gaps and overlaps. A *gap* is a combination of input values for which no rule matches, indicating the table is incomplete. An *overlap* is a combination of input values for which multiple rules match. If incompatible with the hit policy this could indicate an error. We'll discuss Decision Table Analysis in more detail later in the book. Change the table back to the correct entries, shown in Figure 21.

Log Viewer

Severity	Message
❌	Overlap: Rules 4, 5 match with input values [>660, 0.38]. Hit policy U allows only 1 matching rule.
❌	Gap: No rule matches for input values [600, (0.35..0.38)].
❌	Gap: No rule matches for input values [600, 0.35].
❌	Gap: No rule matches for input values [600, 0.38].
❌	Gap: No rule matches for input values [600, <0.35].
❌	Gap: No rule matches for input values [600, >0.38].
❌	Method and Style Validation completed with 6 errors on 1 decision table.

Showing 1 to 7 of 7 entries

Figure 23. Decision Table Analysis reveals gaps and overlaps

The *Validate* button on the DMN ribbon performs additional checks that the model as entered is executable. You should always make sure that your model is valid. Since it is, we are now ready to test it by entering values and seeing if the result is reasonable.

On the Execution ribbon, click Test. A form will appear in which you enter values for the input data, *Credit Score* and *DTI*. Enter *Credit Score* 660 and *DTI* 0.36 and click Run. You should see a value of "Declined", and if you go to the *Loan Approval* page you see exactly which rule matched, here rule 2 (Figure 24).

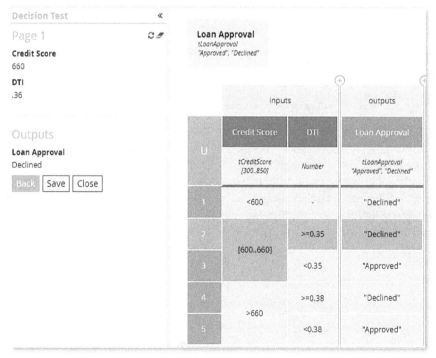

Figure 24. Decision model execution test

Now click the circular arrows in the input panel, change the *Credit Score* to 661, and run again. This time we get "Approved" based on rule 5.

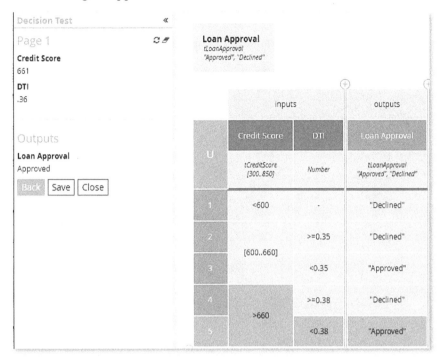

Figure 25. Slightly different input values change the decision outcome

Click the Save button at the bottom of the test panel to save these input and output values as a test case for future reference. If your Trisotech instance is so configured, you can now publish your model as an executable decision service.[16] Simply click Cloud Publish and your decision model is available for execution as a REST call from any external client application or process. Who says DMN is too hard for business users?

Figure 26. Cloud Publish instantly deploys the model as an executable decision service

---

[16] This is not supported in the free trial edition. Contact support@trisotech.com to discuss obtaining access to cloud execution.

CHAPTER 3

Decision Requirements

The notion that a piece of decision logic, such as a decision table, depends on the output of other supporting decisions is not new with DMN. It goes back decades. Vanthienen[17] points to the cover of the 1982 CODASYL report on decision tables (Figure 27), which shows links between a decision table and its supporting decisions.

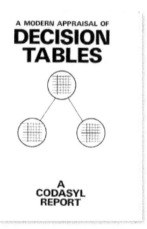

Figure 27. Hierarchy of supporting decisions is nothing new. Source: CODASYL[18]

DMN carries this idea forward in the form of *decision requirements*. A *Decision Requirements Graph* (DRG) and its visual representation, the *Decision Requirements Diagram* (DRD), describe a decision's dependencies on supporting decisions and input data. Those dependencies are described in the form of *information requirements*, solid arrow connectors linking a decision to

[17] Jan Vanthienen, "History of Modeling Decisions using Tables (Part 1)," http://www.brcommunity.com/pb637.php

[18] Codasyl, "A Modern Appraisal of Decision Tables," Report of the Decision Table Task Group, ACM, New York, 322 pp., 1982.

the output of a supporting decision or input data element. Every decision or input data element contains a *variable* having the same name, and the value expression of a decision may reference only variables corresponding to that decision's information requirements.

DMN's representation of decision requirements is borrowed from *The Decision Model*, by von Halle and Goldberg[19], and *Knowledge Automation* by Alan Fish of FICO[20]. FICO's methodology, called Decision Model Analysis, starts with a Decision Requirements Diagram:

> "You can discover the requirements of a decision by asking *what information is required* to make the decision. Information is of three kinds:
>
> 1. Business knowledge (in all its forms: business rules and their metaphors, algorithms, and analytic models)
> 2. Data describing the case to be decided on
> 3. The results of other decisions
>
> The last point is the key: Decisions depend on subdecisions. This allows decision-making to be decomposed into a network that can be drawn in a Decision Requirements Diagram (DRD)."

Decision Requirements Diagram

In DMN, a DRD is a diagram that captures the relationships between a decision and its supporting decisions, business knowledge models, and input data, as well as the knowledge sources (also called authorities) behind the decision logic. The basic DRD element types are shown in Figure 28.

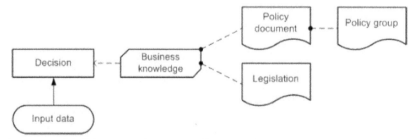

Figure 28. Decision Requirements Diagram elements. Source: OMG

- A *decision* (rectangle) represents decision logic that returns an output value for a given set of input values. It may either directly contain the decision logic or invoke the decision logic specified in an attached business knowledge model.

---

[19] Barbara von Halle and Larry Goldberg, *The Decision Model* (Boca Raton: Taylor and Francis, 2010), http://www.amazon.com/dp/1420082817/

[20] Alan Fish, *Knowledge Automation* (Wiley 2012), https://www.amazon.com/ dp/111809476X

- *Input data* (oval shape) represents data values received at the time of execution. Input data has no value expression.

- A *business knowledge model* (rectangle with two clipped corners) represents a self-contained bit of decision logic. Its value expression is a *function definition*, an expression of its *parameters*. A decision *invokes* a BKM by mapping its inputs to the BKM parameters; the BKM output value is then returned to the invoking decision.

- A *knowledge source* (rectangle with wavy bottom) represents the *authority* for some bit of decision logic. It could be a document, such as a published policy; an external model, such as predictive analytics; or a person, such as a domain expert. Knowledge sources have no execution semantics. They simply document the source of the information used in the decision logic.

The dependencies between decisions, business knowledge models, input data, and knowledge sources are shown graphically as *connectors* called *requirements*:

- The *information requirement* connector, solid arrow, represents the dependency of a decision on a supporting decision or input data.

- The *knowledge requirement* connector, dashed arrow, represents the invocation of a business knowledge model or decision service by a decision or another business knowledge model.

- The *authority requirement* connector, dashed line with dot, represents the dependency of a decision, business knowledge model, or knowledge source on a knowledge source.

The semantic model of *all* a decision's requirements is called its *Decision Requirements Graph* (DRG). Its diagrammatic representation in one or more DRDs, each possibly representing just a partial view of the DRG, may omit certain details. The spec says the DRG is "self-contained in the sense that all the modeled requirements for any Decision in the DRG (its immediate sources of information, knowledge and authority) are present in the same DRG."

Also, the DRG must be "acyclic," meaning if *Decision A* depends on *Decision B* (directly or indirectly), then *Decision B* may not depend on *Decision A*. Another way of saying it is there should be no chain of information requirements leading from *Decision A* and cycling back to *Decision A*.

Modeling Decision Requirements

Decision modeling in DMN generally starts by modeling the decision requirements as one or more DRDs. Even without specifying the value expressions of its decision nodes, the DRD on its own reveals a good deal about the logic of a business decision. It tells you what input data you need (and don't need), as well as the logical subdecisions required. Moreover, as it is simply a diagram, it easily engages business stakeholders in the project.

While it does not normally show up in the DRD, an important part of decision requirements modeling is specifying the *types* of each decision and input data node, in particular when they are based on *item definitions* specifying its allowed values. Together with these type definitions, the DRD provides a complete specification of decision requirements that can be handed off to developers for implementation in any decision language. Of course, it's always best to have that implementation done in DMN, as that fosters continuous business-IT collaboration throughout the project lifecycle.

Decision Requirements by Example

Let's see how this works in a tool like the Trisotech DMN Modeler. Again we'll focus on a lending example, this time a mortgage loan prequalification decision, such as might appear on the lender's website to give prospective borrowers an idea of the likelihood of approval based on credit score, loan amount, and income. We start by dragging out a top-level decision and labeling it *Loan prequalification*.

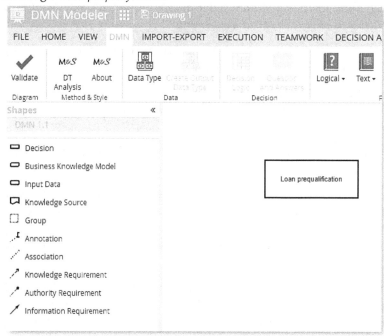

Figure 29. Top-level decision in the DRD

Any decision element in the DRD, but especially the top one, should be documented as a question and allowed answers, typically an enumerated list of values. The question and allowed answers are actually standard elements in the DMN metamodel and interchange XML. Trisotech provides a simple dialog to enter them (Figure 30). In this case the question is, "Based on self-reported borrower income, credit score, loan amount, what is the likely eligibility for a mortgage?" with possible answers "Likely approved", "Possibly approved", and "Likely disapproved".

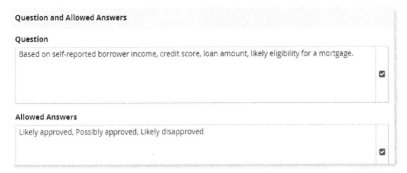

Figure 30. Question and Allowed Answers

These allowed values actually define the datatype of *Loan prequalification*. To enter that in the model, right-click the decision shape in the DRD and select Output data type/New type and name it *tLoanPrequalification*. Select type Text with Constraint type Enumeration, and enter the enumerated values (Figure 31).

Figure 31. Allowed answers determine the datatype

You've now created an item definition, *tLoanPrequalification*, a named type with three enumerated values, and assigned it to the decision.

Figure 32. Item definition specifies allowed values

Next we consider what data must be provided in order to evaluate this decision. It could be as simple as just the three elements mentioned earlier – credit score, income, and loan amount – but in this case we'll use five elements: *Credit score, Monthly income, Purchase price, Down payment, and Loan rate pct.* Drag these out as input data.

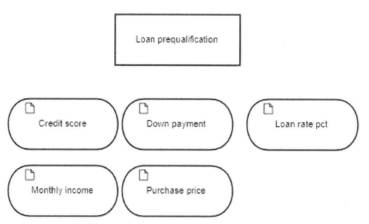

Figure 33. Add input data to the DRD

We can define the type of each input by right-click Attributes/Input data type. *Credit score* is a number from 300 to 850 inclusive, so define a new type *tCreditScore*, type Number, constraint type Simple, min 300, max 850 inclusive. *Loan rate pct* is a number, but expressed as a percent, so a loan rate of 0.041 would have a *Loan rate pct* value of 4.1. To remind us of this, we assign it to the new type *tPercent*, base type Number and no constraints. The other three we'll make a new type *tPositiveNumber*, type Number, simple constraint, min 0 exclusive.

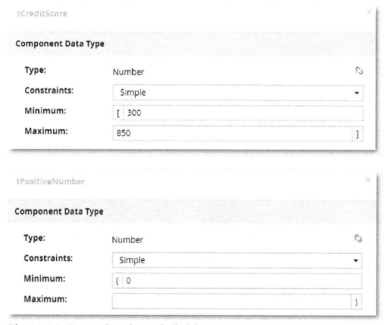

Figure 34. Input data item definitions

The DMN spec describes no standard visualization of the type assignment, but Trisotech allows you to see it as a DRD overlay (Figure 35). It's a good idea to check that all elements have types defined.

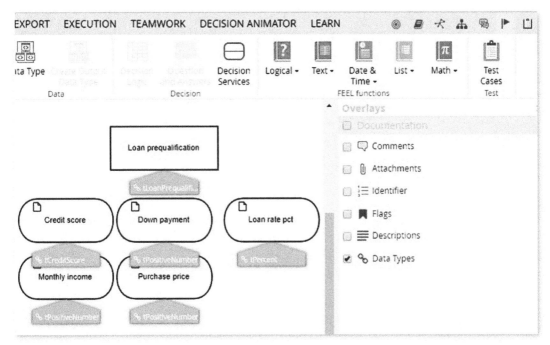

Figure 35. Visualizing datatype assignment

Our subject matter experts tell us that *Loan prequalification* really depends on two factors: the *Credit score* and whether the loan is affordable, as measured by the ratio of the loan payment to monthly income. We'll call the latter *Affordability category* and assign it to a new type, *tAffordabilityCategory*, with enumerated values "Affordable", "Marginal", and "Unaffordable" (Figure 36). In the DRD, that means those are the two information requirements of *Loan prequalification* (Figure 37).

Figure 36. Supporting decision type definition

We know the loan payment is based on some combination of the *Purchase price, Down payment,* and *Loan rate pct.* Drawing the information requirements, our DRD now looks like this:

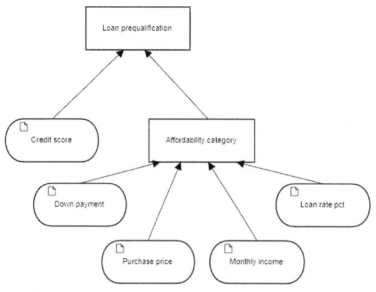

Figure 37. DRD with supporting decision

In Figure 38, a *knowledge source,* the wavy-bottom shape, is an optional graphical annotation of the DRD used to represent the source of the decision logic or its elements. This could be company policies, regulations, analytics, or simply the opinion of a subject matter expert. It is linked to the DRD element it annotates via a dashed connector called an *authority requirement.* In a DMN tool, clicking on the knowledge source typically displays the associated documentation.

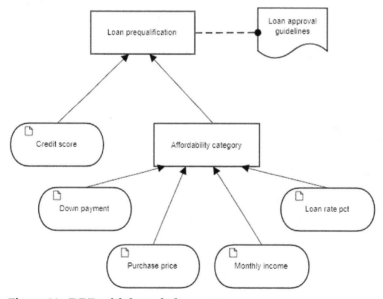

Figure 38. DRD with knowledge source

For example, here the knowledge source *Loan approval guidelines* provides information about the *Loan prequalification* decision. In Trisotech DMN Modeler, you can specify knowledge source details including a description, documentation and comments, the owner, type, and a web link (Figure 39).

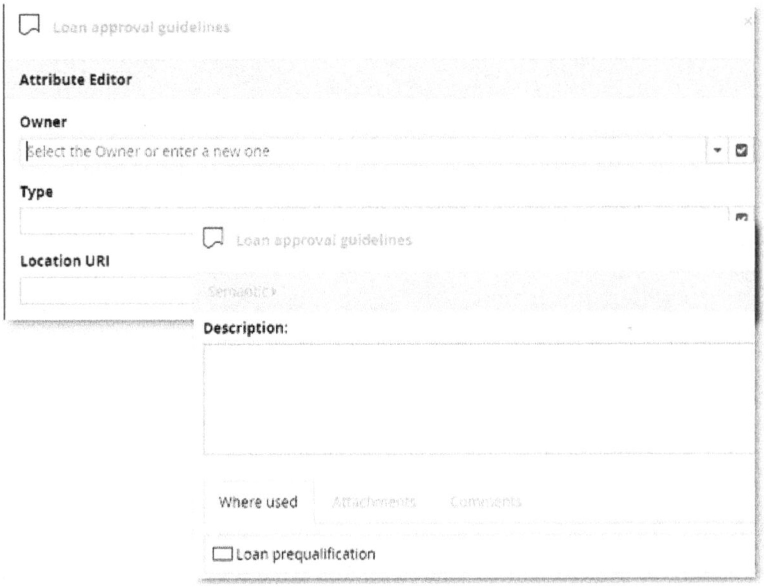

Figure 39. Knowledge source details

Affordability category classifies values of the debt-to-income ratio as "Affordable", "Marginal", or "Unaffordable". This ratio is defined as the housing expense divided by the borrower's monthly income, where housing expense is the monthly loan payment plus the estimated monthly tax and insurance payments.

In the DRD we just care about the names of the inputs and their types, not the value expression calculations. So in our DRD we say *Affordability category* depends on a supporting decision *DTI pct*, type *tPercent*, which in turn depends on supporting decision *Housing expense*, type *tPositiveNumber*, and input data *Monthly income*. *Housing expense* depends on supporting decisions *Tax and insurance payment* and *Loan payment*, both type *tPositiveNumber*. *Loan payment* in turn depends on supporting decision *Loan amount*, type *tPositiveNumber*, and input data *Loan rate pct*, where *Loan amount* depends on the input data *Purchase price* and *Down payment*.

With all of that, we can now complete the Decision Requirements Diagram (Figure 40).

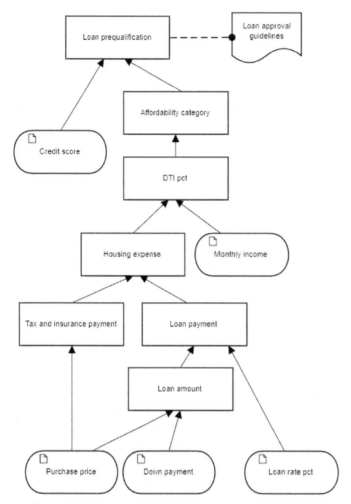

Figure 40. The complete DRD

Even without defining the value expressions of any of the decision nodes, Figure 40 in combination with the assigned datatypes provides a complete outline of the end-to-end decision logic. Two of the elements – *Loan prequalification* and *Affordability category* – are classification decisions using decision tables. All the others are essentially arithmetic calculations. We can hand off this DRD to a more technical modeler for implementation, i.e., completion of the value expressions. But since this logic is simple, most business users can actually do it themselves.

CHAPTER 4

Basic Decision Logic

As we saw in the previous chapter, even without defining the value expressions, the DRD provides detailed requirements for implementation. But DMN provides more than just decision requirements. It is a language that allows non-technical users to define a good portion of the decision logic themselves, and not only define it, but validate and test it as well, even deploy it as an executable decision service.

Doing that requires specifying the value expression for each decision node in the DRD, the rules and formulas that transform the values of each decision's inputs to its output value. DMN standardizes various tabular formats, called *boxed expressions*, that define these rules and formulas. Any business user should be able to master the three most basic expression types: *decision tables*, logic based on rules; *literal expressions*, formulas such as arithmetic; and *invocations*, leveraging decision logic created by others.

In this chapter, we continue the previous example to get started with that.

Decision Table Basics

It's not required, but I generally start at the top of the DRD, in this case the top-level decision *Loan prequalification*. We know from the DRD its inputs are *Credit score*, a number, and *Affordability category*, which is either "Affordable", "Marginal", or "Unaffordable", and the decision output must be either "Likely approved", "Possibly approved", or "Likely disapproved". Classification decisions like this one generally use a decision table.

In Trisotech DMN Modeler, when we select the expression type Decision Table for *Loan prequalification*, the tool fills in the table inputs and output and their types (Figure 41). We just need to enter the rules.

Loan prequalification
tLoanPrequalification
"Likely approved", "Possibly approved", "Likely disapproved"

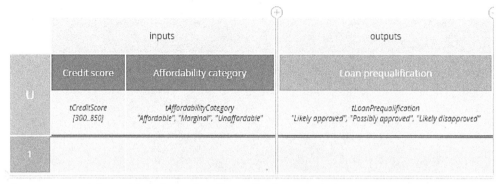

	inputs		outputs
	Credit score	**Affordability category**	**Loan prequalification**
U	*tCreditScore* [300..850]	*tAffordabilityCategory* "Affordable", "Marginal", "Unaffordable"	*tLoanPrequalification* "Likely approved", "Possibly approved", "Likely disapproved"
1			

Figure 41. Decision table column headings display type information

Our SMEs tell us a credit score below 620 is poor, 620-680 is fair, 680-720 is good, and over 720 is excellent. Now we could have added a supporting decision with these named output values, but here we will just use the numeric ranges directly in our logic. The SMEs tell us that the loan is likely approved if the credit score is excellent and affordability is either affordable or marginal, and also likely approved if the credit score is good and the loan is affordable. It is possibly approved if credit score is good and affordability marginal, or credit score is fair and affordable. And it is likely disapproved if the credit score is fair and affordability marginal, or either credit score is poor or affordability unaffordable.

So we need to enter those rules in the table. Each condition cell, or *input entry*, in a rule, when combined with the column heading, or *input expression*, creates a Boolean condition, true or false. A rule *matches* if all its condition cells have a true condition, and in that case its *output entry* value is selected. The datatype shown in each column heading shows the allowed values of the input expression and output entry.

Applying the guidance of the SMEs results in the table shown in Figure 42. Note that we used derived categories for affordability and raw values for credit score. We could have used derived categories for both, or raw numbers for both. We'll talk about the advantages of using derived classifications later in the training, but in a decision table we can use them or not.

Suppose some instance of this decision has *Credit score* less than 620 and *Affordability category* of "Unaffordable". In that case both rules 6 and 7 match. Hit policy U, the default, does not allow that, so we need to change the hit policy to A, for Any. This says that overlapping rules – meaning both match for certain input values – are allowed if they both have the same output value... and here they do, "Likely disapproved".

A	Credit score	Affordability category	Loan prequalification
	tCreditScore [300..850]	tAffordabilityCategory "Affordable", "Marginal", "Unaffordable"	tLoanPrequalification "Likely approved", "Possibly approved", "Likely disapproved"
1	>720	"Affordable", "Marginal"	"Likely approved"
2	(680..720]	"Affordable"	"Likely approved"
3	(680..720]	"Marginal"	"Possibly approved"
4	[620..680]	"Affordable"	"Possibly approved"
5	[620..680]	"Marginal"	"Likely disapproved"
6	<620	-	"Likely disapproved"
7	-	"Unaffordable"	"Likely disapproved"

Figure 42. Decision table before cell merging

Note that rules 2 and 3 have the same input entry for Credit score, as do rules 4 and 5. In that case DMN allows you to merge those condition cells, which some experts say makes the table easier to read. Figure 43 shows what that looks like in Trisotech DMN Modeler.

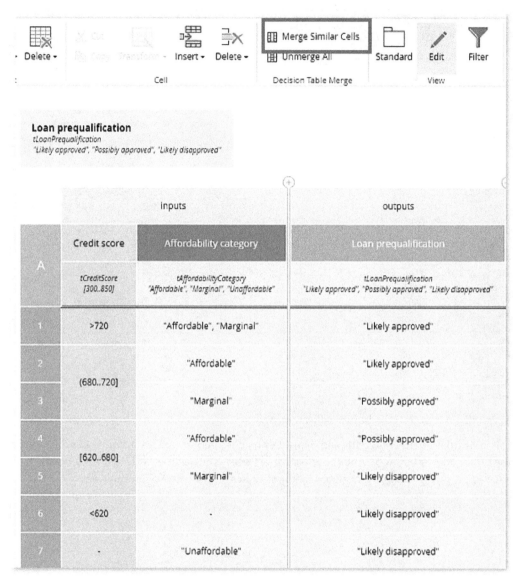

Figure 43. Decision table with cell merging

What Can You Put in a Decision Table Condition Cell?

The reason it's easy to understand and analyze the logic of a decision table is that DMN strongly limits what you can put in a condition cell, or input entry.

- If the input is a number, like *Credit score*, we can enter a *number*, testing whether the input value is *equal* to that number; or a *comparison*, such as greater than that number, or less than or equal to that number; or a *range* with minimum and maximum values separated by two dots. The symbols bracketing the range define whether the endpoints are included: Square bracket means included, parenthesis means excluded. Thus in Figure 43 rules 2 and 3, the first column tests whether *Credit score* is greater than 680 and less than or equal to 720.

- If the input is an enumerated value, the input entry may be a literal value, like rule 2 "Affordable", or a comma-separated list of literal values, like rule 1, meaning is the *Affordability category* either "Affordable" or "Marginal". Note that literal text values are enclosed in double quotes. That's required in a FEEL literal expression. In an input entry, if you leave off the quotes, it means a *variable* with that name, and if you do that by accident, the tool will try to correct your error by wrapping it in quotes.

- Literal values of dates and times behave like numbers, with comparisons and ranges. However, dates, times, and durations must be entered using a *constructor function*, such as date("2017-02-14"), with the date written as a text value in a particular format, enclosed in quotes, inside parentheses preceded by the function name *date*. The spec says that in a decision table or other boxed expression, literal text values may be displayed in italics without the quotes, and date-time literals may be displayed in bold italics without the constructor function or quotes.

- Input entries are not required to reference numbers or literal text values. They may reference a variable *name* as long as that variable is a valid input to the decision, meaning the DRD shows an information requirement from a node with that name pointing to the decision.

- For any input type, you can always enter *hyphen* in the condition cell, meaning the input is irrelevant in this rule.

- If you want to have a rule with the condition "if *Affordability category* is not equal to 'Unaffordable'," you would enter not("Unaffordable"). Actually, *not()* is the *only* expression other than a simple value or name that is allowed in an input entry. Even simple arithmetic expressions are not allowed.

Collectively, these constraints on input entries are called *unary tests*. Restricting condition cells to unary tests is a distinguishing feature of DMN decision tables. The unary tests constraint delivers a huge benefit, as it makes it possible for the tool to check the table for completeness, consistency, and other best modeling practices. We'll see how this works later when we discuss Decision Table Analysis.

Because other decision languages do not have such constraints, several decision modeling vendors considering DMN complained to the standards committee and requested relaxing the unary tests rule. As a result, DMN 1.2 did that, allowing what are called *generalized unary tests*. Generalized unary tests effectively allow any FEEL expression in a condition cell, with the ? character substituting for the input expression. Although the resulting rules are very flexible, the syntax is not business-friendly.

The output column of a decision rule is not restricted to unary tests. You can enter any FEEL expression that evaluates to an allowed value.

Example: Affordability category

Recall that the decision *Affordability category* merely classifies *DTI pct*, a number expressed as percent, into three possible values: "Affordable", "Marginal", and "Unaffordable". The rules are these:

- "Affordable" if *DTI pct* is less than 26.

- "Marginal" if *DTI pct* is between 26 and 28, including the endpoints.

- "Unaffordable" if *DTI pct* is greater than 28.

The table looks like this:

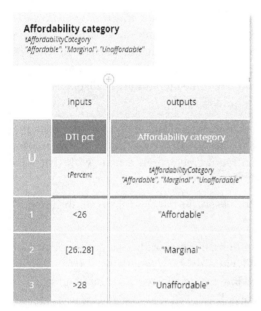

Figure 44. Decision logic for *Affordability category*

Literal Expressions

Computations and other expressions that do not involve conditional logic typically do not use decision tables. Instead they use *literal expressions*, formulas written as text expressions in FEEL. FEEL is the standard expression language of DMN. It is a pure expression language, not a full programming language. It does not normally create variables, but simply returns a value. FEEL is designed to be business-friendly but at the same time executable on an engine. It is actually quite powerful, containing many built-in functions and operators. Some of these, admittedly, may be difficult for some business users to understand. The ones we'll talk about here, however, are simple arithmetic.

The decision *DTI pct* is an example. It is simply the *Housing expense* divided by *Monthly income*, and because we want this fraction expressed as a percent, we need to multiply it by 100.

Figure 45. Literal expression in Trisotech expression editor

Figure 45 shows this literal expression in the official boxed expression format, with the decision name in a tab at the top and the expression text underneath. The code F at the right denotes this as a FEEL expression, as opposed to natural language, unparsed and not executable. Because these expressions are executable, they must follow the syntax rules of the language exactly. To help with this, the Trisotech DMN Modeler suggests names of valid names as you type and turns valid variable names purple. An entered name that is not recognized as a valid input is assumed to be a literal value and wrapped in quotes automatically.

Housing expense, also simple arithmetic, is another literal expression (Figure 46).

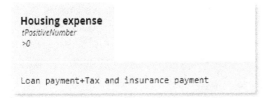

Figure 46. Literal expression for *Housing expense*

Tax and insurance payment depends on the *Purchase price*. In a more realistic model, it also depends on the property location, as the tax rate and insurance costs vary by location, but here we will just use "typical" values for the USA, where the average annual property tax is 1.25% of the purchase price and the average annual homeowner insurance premium is $3.50 per $1000 of purchase price. We want the monthly value, so we divide by 12 (Figure 47)

Figure 47. Literal expression for *Tax and insurance payment*

BKMs and Invocation

Loan payment calculates the monthly loan payment based on the *Loan amount* and the *Loan rate pct*. The formula is just arithmetic, so we could make it a literal expression, but it is a complicated formula, hard to remember and easy to type in wrong. Fortunately, it is a formula – the Loan Amortization Formula – used all the time in lending calculations, so someone in our organization has already modeled it and saved it in a library for reuse as a *business knowledge model*, or *BKM*.

In the DRD, a BKM is represented as a rectangle with two clipped corners, connected to a decision by a dashed arrow connector called a *knowledge requirement*. BKMs have no information requirements, the solid arrows. Instead, BKMs define their own inputs, called *parameters*. The BKM's value expression – which could be a decision table, literal expression, or invocation – can only reference its parameters.

The knowledge requirement connector signifies *invocation* of the BKM by a decision (or possibly by another BKM). The boxed invocation defines how the inputs of the invoking decision are mapped to the BKM parameters. Upon execution, the decision transforms its input values to BKM parameter values, calls the BKM value expression, and receives its output value in return.

BKMs are inherently *reusable*, since any decision needing that bit of decision logic can invoke it by mapping its inputs to the BKM parameters. The creator of the BKM does not need to know the names of the variables in the models that invoke it.

Let's see how all this works in the context of *Loan payment*. Using the tool, we can copy and paste the *Loan Amortization Formula* BKM from a library and drop it into our model (Figure 48). (In this case we are just pasting in a *copy*, which we could edit if we want; there is also a way to *import* a non-editable *reference* to the BKM, which we will discuss later in the book.)

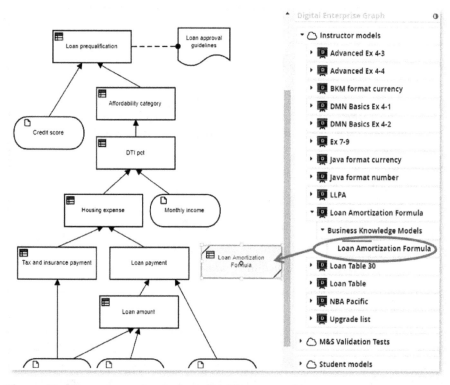

Figure 48. Element copy/paste from the Places panel

If we inspect the BKM's decision logic (Figure 49), we see it is a literal expression of three parameters, p, r, and n, all numbers. As promised, it is just arithmetic, but complicated. The symbol ** in FEEL means "raised to the power".

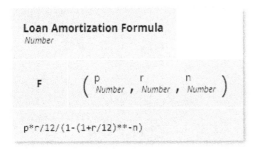

Loan Amortization Formula
Number

F $\left(\begin{array}{ccc} p & r & n \\ Number & , & Number & , & Number \end{array}\right)$

p*r/12/(1-(1+r/12)**-n)

Figure 49. *Loan Amortization Formula* **BKM**

It is important that the BKM's creator has documented its parameters and usage so that it can be properly understood by those who would invoke it. In this case (Figure 50), we see that p is the loan amount, r is the annual loan rate expressed as a decimal (not percent), and n is the number of months in the loan term.

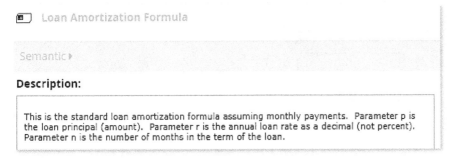

Loan Amortization Formula

Semantic ▸

Description:

This is the standard loan amortization formula assuming monthly payments. Parameter p is the loan principal (amount). Parameter r is the annual loan rate as a decimal (not percent). Parameter n is the number of months in the term of the loan.

Figure 50. BKM documentation explains the parameters and usage

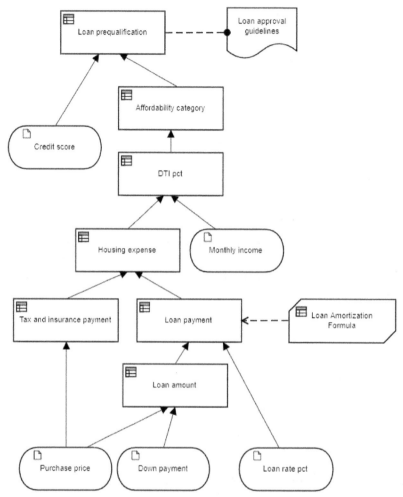

Figure 51. Knowledge requirement connector signifies invocation of BKM

The *knowledge requirement* dashed arrow (Figure 51) signifies that *Loan payment* invokes the BKM and receives its output as a result. The value expression of *Loan payment* is an *invocation*, defined by the tabular format shown in Figure 52. The top row identifies the BKM being invoked. Below that is a two-column table, with the BKM parameters listed on the left, and expressions (typically literal expressions) mapping the inputs of *Loan payment* to each one. Here parameter *p* is just the input *Loan amount*. Because *r* is a decimal and *Loan rate pct* is a percent, we need to divide the latter by 100. We are just working with 30-year fixed rate loans, so *n* is the constant 360.

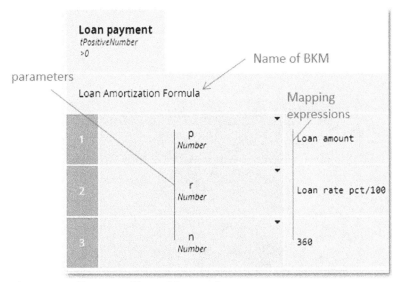

Figure 52. Elemens of boxed invocation

With invocation, we don't have to be able to derive every value expression or even remember how to enter it. All we need to know is how to invoke it. This opens up executable decision modeling to a much wider range of business users.

Test Execution

At this point we have a complete DRD and value expressions for every decision and BKM in it. Any good DMN tool should have a button to validate the model, checking for errors in input references and expression syntax, things that would prevent the model from running. Ideally, the tool can also check decision tables for completeness, consistency, and other best practices, as we will see in Chapter 7.

But those validation checks are not really enough. Just because the model runs doesn't mean it is correct. It is also important to create test cases where you know the answer and see if your model returns the expected result.

For example, in Trisotech DMN Modeler, you can enter values for all the input data elements and click Run to return the values of all decision nodes in the model (Figure 53). If you view a decision table page in the model, you even see which rules matched. It is very easy to make mistakes keying in decision logic, especially numeric formulas, and checking whether the returned values of all the decisions (not just the top level) are reasonable is a prerequisite for success.

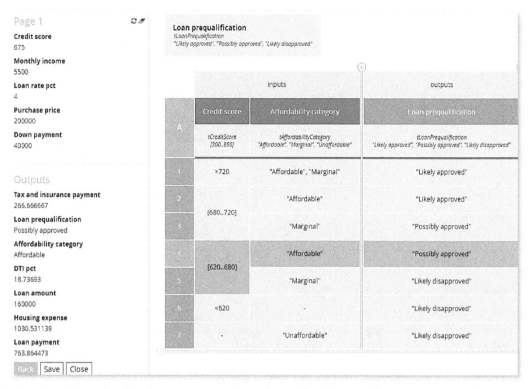

Figure 53. Execution Test/Run returns output for all decisions in the DRD

Trisotech also lets you save sets of input and returned output values as *test cases* that can be shared or used for debugging.

CHAPTER 5

Routing Decisions

A question that often comes up is how decision models in DMN relate to process models in BPMN. In this chapter, we'll see how that works.

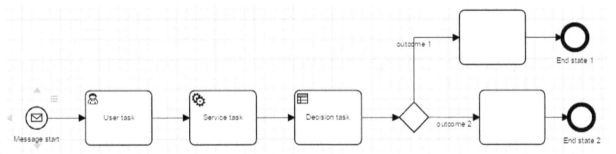

Figure 54. A process model (BPMN)

The diagram you see here is not a decision model in DMN. It is a *process model* in BPMN. BPMN models a business process in the form of sequences of *activities*, the boxes, leading from some initial state of the process, denoted by the *start event*, the thin circle, to some *end state* of the process, denoted by the thick circles.

The diamond shapes in the flow, called *gateways*, represent branch points in the flow. Unlike traditional flowcharting, in BPMN, gateways do not make decisions, they just test data conditions in order to route the activity flow. Each arrow, called a *sequence flow*, outgoing from the gateway is labeled with a condition. The one with a true condition for this instance of the process is the path taken out of the gateway.

An icon in the upper left corner of an activity indicates its type. A *user task* (head and shoulders icon) signifies an activity performed by a person. A *service task* (gears icon) signifies an activity performed automatically. A *decision task* (spreadsheet icon, also called *business rules task*) signifies invocation of a decision modeled in DMN.

When a gateway follows a decision task, the condition label indicates the outcome of the decision, the DMN output value. So if the decision output value is "outcome 1", the process proceeds on the path leading to *End state 1*, and if the decision output value is "outcome 2", it takes the other branch out of the gateway, the one leading to *End state 2*.

Bad BPMN

The diagram of an insurance claims process illustrated in Figure 55 is considered "bad BPMN", because the logic determining whether the claim is automatically denied, routed to an adjudicator for a human decision, or is processed automatically, is modeled as a *chain of gateways*. In decision management, such logic is called a *decision tree*, and it is considered bad practice, both in BPM and decision management, to model a decision tree as a BPMN process.

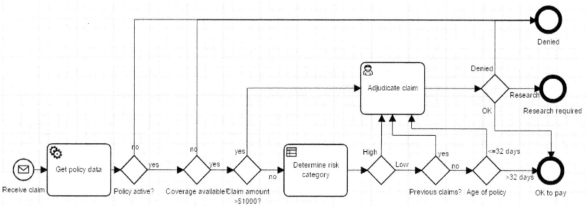

Figure 55. Chained gateways are "bad BPMN"

For one thing, it makes the process logic complicated and hard to understand. It also hides important details of the decision logic, such as what the inputs mean and how they are related. Moreover, it specifies a particular order of evaluating the decision logic that might not be required or even the most efficient in practice. And most important, even a minor change in the routing decision logic requires revising and redeploying a new version of the process. Fortunately, there is a better way to handle this.

Invoking a Routing Decision

It's better to replace a chain of gateways in your process model with a single *decision task* that invokes a *routing decision* modeled in DMN. The decision task is followed by a single gateway with one *gate* – each sequence flow out of a gateway is called a gate – per allowed value of the decision.

Why is this better? For starters, it makes the process logic simpler and easier to follow. The DMN model for the routing decision makes the decision logic transparent, and the decision model does not impose a specific order of evaluation. There is a business agility benefit as well: As long as the allowed output values of the decision remain the same, you can revise the decision logic without revising and redeploying the process model. The routing logic can be changed on the fly.

So let's see how to do this. The process model (Figure 55) says when we receive a claim, first we retrieve data on the customer's policy. If it's not currently active, we immediately deny the claim. If it's active but the claim is not covered under the policy, again we immediately deny. If it's covered and the claim amount is over $1000, we need human adjudication. If it is $1000 or less we apply further decision logic.

Those first three gateways in Figure 55 comprise the decision tree modeled as BPMN. We want to turn it into a single decision task, *Routing 1*, that invokes a DMN model, followed by a single gateway with one gate per decision output value. That is shown in Figure 56. And notice that on the further-processing path there is a second chain of gateways. We want to turn that into a second decision task, *Routing 2*. The process diagram shown in Figure 56 is "good BPMN". Embedded decision trees have been replaced by decision tasks invoking DMN decisions, followed by gateways with one gate per DMN output value.

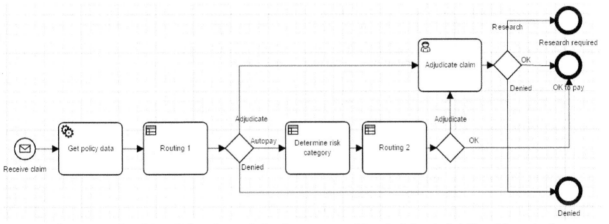

Figure 56. "Good BPMN" replaces chained gateways with a decision task followd by a single gateway

Routing Decision Logic

Process model transformations like the one from Figure 55 to Figure 56 are extremely simple to construct, following a straightforward procedure.

Let's start with *Routing 1*. First question: What are its possible output values? Remember, with routing decisions each output value corresponds to a gate in the gateway following the decision task in BPMN. So the question we want to ask is, how many gates are there, and what do they correspond to?

In BPMN, each gate corresponds to a *different next step* in the process, so from Figure 55, let's count them.

1.   One next step is the end state *Denied*.

2.   A second next step is the human task *Adjudicate claim*.

3. And a third next step is the decision task *Determine risk category*, the start of the "further decision logic". There are no other possible next steps.

Three possible next steps means there are three gates following the decision task. We need to name them, so let's call them *Denied, Adjudicate,* and *Autopay*. By default, those become the three possible output values of the *Routing1* decision in DMN.

Those are the outputs. The chain of gateways in Figure 55 give us the inputs and the rules. The implied inputs are:

- *Is Policy Active,* a Boolean;
- *Is Coverage Available,* another Boolean;
- *Claim amount,* a number.

Those are the input data required by *Routing 1* in DMN, so we can create a decision model for the *Routing 1* decision with those inputs. We create a DRD and assign types to *Routing 1* and the input data, and proceed to model the value expression as a decision table. As we've learned from the previous chapter, the tool is going to initialize the table as in Figure 57.

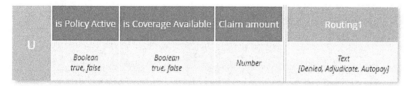

	is Policy Active	is Coverage Available	Claim amount	Routing1
U	Boolean true, false	Boolean true, false	Number	Text [Denied, Adjudicate, Autopay]

Figure 57. *Routing1* **inputs and output**

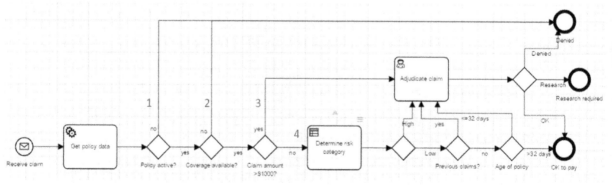

Figure 58. Routing decision rules determined from the original BPMN

The original process model (Figure 58) tells us the rules:

1. If *is Policy Active* = false then "Denied"

2. If *is Policy Active* = true and *is Coverage Available* = false then "Denied"

3. If *is Policy Active* = true and *is Coverage Available* = true and *Claim Amount* >1000 then "Adjudicate"

---

4. If *is Policy Active* = true and *is Coverage Available* = true and *Claim Amount* <=1000 then "Autopay"

Those rules are directly implemented in the decision table (Figure 59).

U	is Policy Active	is Coverage Available	Claim amount	Routing1
	Boolean true, false	Boolean true, false	Number	Text [Denied, Adjudicate, Autopay]
1	false	-	-	"Denied"
2	true	false	-	"Denied"
3	true	true	>1000	"Adjudicate"
4	true	true	<=1000	"Autopay"

Figure 59. *Routing1* **logic as a decision table**

In the same way, we can derive Routing 2 from the original BPMN (Figure 60).

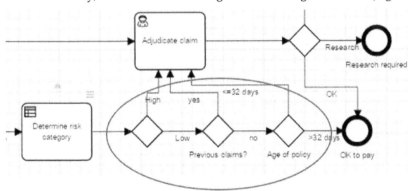

Figure 60. Source of *Routing2* **logic**

We see there are two possible next steps: the end state *OK to pay* and the activity *Adjudicate claim*, so we name the output values of *Routing 2* "OK" and "Adjudicate". The inputs are *Risk Category,* with possible values "High" and "Low"; *has Previous Claims,* a Boolean; and *Age Days,* a number. As before, the process diagram tells us the rules, which we translate directly into the *Routing 2* decision table (Figure 61). Direct translation of the process logic gives us a table with hit policy U, but we can often turn it into an A table with slightly simpler logic (Figure 62). We discuss hit policy in more depth in the next chapter.

U	Risk Category	has Previous Claims	Age Days	Routing2
	Text [High, Low]	Boolean true, false	Number	Text [OK, Adjudicate]
1	"High"	-	-	"Adjudicate"
2	"Low"	true	-	"Adjudicate"
3	"Low"	false	<=32	"Adjudicate"
4	"Low"	false	>32	"OK"

Figure 61. *Routing2* logic as a decision table

A	Risk Category	has Previous Claims	Age Days	Routing2
	Text [High, Low]	Boolean true, false	Number	Text [OK, Adjudicate]
1	"High"	-	-	"Adjudicate"
2	-	true	-	"Adjudicate"
3	-	-	<=32	"Adjudicate"
4	"Low"	false	>32	"OK"

Figure 62. Hit policy A makes a simpler decision table

CHAPTER 6

Decision Table Hit Policy

Handling ORed Conditions

A decision table's *hit policy* sounds mysterious but really is not hard to understand. The right hit policy can make your decision tables easier to create and understand, but you can make mistakes with hit policy as well.

Recall that in a decision table rule, the conditions on each column are always ANDed together:

```
If condition1=true AND condition2=true AND... conditionN=true then "X"
```

In that case, how would you model the following logic for *Offer eligibility*?

```
If Customer category="Gold" or Order amount>=1000 then "Eligible"
else "Ineligible"
```

Here the conditions for "Eligible" are ORed together, so you cannot model this as a single decision rule. Instead you need *two rules*, like this:

	Customer category	Order amount	Offer eligibility
U	tCustomerCategory "Gold", "Silver", "None"	Number	tOfferEligibility "Eligible", "Ineligible"
1	"Gold"	-	"Eligible"
2	-	>=1000	"Eligible"
3	"Silver","None"	<1000	"Ineligible"

Figure 63. ORed conditions require separate decision table rules

Actually, this table is not completely correct, because if *Customer category*="Gold" and *Order amount*>=1000, both rules 1 and 2 match, and the default hit policy U, for Unique, says that only one rule may match any combination of input values. In Trisotech DMN Modeler, if you run Decision Table Analysis, the tool tells you this:

Log Viewer

Severity	Message
☒	Overlap: Rules 1, 2 match with input values ["Gold", >=1000]. Hit policy U allows only 1 matching rule.

Figure 64. Hit policy U does not allow overlapping rules

When it is possible that some combination of input values causes more than one rule to match, those rules are said to *overlap*. A decision table's hit policy specifies the table output value when rules overlap. Hit policy U says rules may not overlap.

In Figure 63, rules 1 and 2 overlap, but both have the same output value "Eligible". In that case the correct hit policy is A, for Any. Hit policy A says rules may overlap if they have the same output value, so the decision table shown in Figure 65 is correct.

A	Customer category	Order amount	Offer eligibility
	tCustomerCategory "Gold", "Silver", "None"	Number	tOfferEligibility "Eligible", "Ineligible"
1	"Gold"	-	"Eligible"
2	-	>=1000	"Eligible"
3	"Silver","None"	<1000	"Ineligible"

Figure 65. Hit policy A allows overlapping rules with same output value

Hit Policy Overview

Here is a summary of all DMN hit policies.

- We just discussed U and A. U means rules may not overlap; any combination of inputs can match at most one rule. A means overlapping rules are allowed, but they must have the same output value.

- Hit policy P, for Priority, is one we use a lot. It allows rules with different output values to overlap and selects the value with the highest *priority*. The priority order is determined by the order of listed output values in the output column heading. P tables only work when the output column enumerates its allowed values. We'll talk later about two different styles of Priority tables that I call P1 and P2.

- Hit policy F, for First, is one I don't use at all. It also allows rules with different output values to overlap and selects the output of the first matching rule. However, hit policy F violates a long-held principle of decision management that the order of rules in the table should not matter to the result. That principle, called *declarative logic*, is not required by the DMN spec but is considered best practice, and I always ask students to use a P table instead of an F table.

- Hit policies U, A, P, and F select a single output value, but other hit policies collect the outputs of all matching rules in a list. Hit policy C, for Collect, does just this, but does not specify the ordering of the list. Hit policy C also supports optional *aggregation* attributes – sum (+), count (#), maximum (>), and minimum (<). Of these by far the most common is C+, meaning collect and sum, applicable to numeric outputs.

- Variants of hit policy C are O and R. O means collect and list in priority order, like hit policy P. R means collect and list in rule order, like hit policy F. Both are very rarely used; in fact I've never seen either one in the wild.

A Tables Often Simpler than U Tables

In decision logic with ORed conditions, A tables are often simpler to construct and understand than U tables. For example, consider the rule

> If *Credit risk category* is "High" or *Affordability category* is "Unaffordable" then *Loan approval* is "Declined" else "Approved"

Although it is always possible to construct a U table equivalent to any A table, the A table (Figure 66) is simpler to create and to understand than the corresponding U table (Figure 67), which must ensure that any combination of input values matches only one rule.

A	Credit risk category	Affordability category	Loan approval
	tCreditRiskCategory "High", "Medium", "Low"	tAffordabilityCategory "Affordable", "Marginal", "Unaffordable"	tLoanApproval "Approved", "Declined"
1	"High"	-	"Declined"
2	-	"Unaffordable"	"Declined"
3	"Medium", "Low"	"Affordable", "Marginal"	"Approved"

Figure 66. A table often simpler than corresponding U table

U	Credit risk category	Affordability category	Loan approval
	tCreditRiskCategory "High", "Medium", "Low"	tAffordabilityCategory "Affordable", "Marginal", "Unaffordable"	tLoanApproval "Approved", "Declined"
1	"High"	-	"Declined"
2	"Medium", "Low"	"Unaffordable"	"Declined"
3	"Medium", "Low"	"Affordable", "Marginal"	"Approved"

Figure 67. U table equivalent to Figure 66

Hit Policy P

For some decisions, hit policy P, for Priority, provides even simpler decision tables than hit policy A. With hit policy P, overlapping rules may have different output values. The value selected is the one with the highest *priority*, determined by the order the values are listed in the output column heading. The first one listed is the highest priority, the next one is the second priority, etc. So P tables only make sense with enumerated output values.

With P tables you must be aware of the priority order of the output values, which typically is determined when you define the datatype. If you want to change it, you need to edit the datatype.

P	Credit risk category	Affordability category	Loan approval
	tCreditRiskCategory "High", "Medium", "Low"	tAffordabilityCategory "Affordable", "Marginal", "Unaffordable"	tLoanApproval "Declined", "Approved"
1	"High"	-	"Declined"
2	-	"Unaffordable"	"Declined"
3	-	-	"Approved"

Figure 68. P table prioritizes rules based on order of allowed values

Figure 68 is the same decision logic as the previous decision tables, but with hit policy P. It is simpler than the A or U tables because rule 3, the "else" rule, is all hyphens. A rule with hyphen for all input entries always matches, but if its output value is the lowest priority – which it must be – it is only selected if none of the other (higher priority) rules match. In this way, an all-hyphen rule in a P table represents the "else" or "otherwise" condition, simplifying the logic. For that reason, a P table often requires fewer rules than the equivalent U or A table.

With simple either-or logic as in this decision, there are two different forms of P tables. I call them P1 and P2, although there is no such designation in the spec. Figure 68 is the P1 variant, similar to the A table (Figure 66), but slightly simpler, since rule 3 is all hyphens.

P	Credit risk category	Affordability category	Loan approval
	tCreditRiskCategory "High", "Medium", "Low"	tAffordabilityCategory "Affordable", "Marginal", "Unaffordable"	tLoanApproval "Approved", "Declined"
1	"Medium", "Low"	"Affordable", "Marginal"	"Approved"
2	-	-	"Declined"

Figure 69. P2 variant of the P table

Figure 69 is the P2 variant, which is even simpler, with only two rules. Note that the "else" output is different in the two tables. "Approved" is the else rule output in the P1 table, and "Declined" is the else rule output in the P2 table. To create the P2 table, we had to flip the order of the values of *tLoanApproval*.

Which way is best, P1 or P2? Both forms have their advantages. The P1 table (Figure 68) expresses the logic more clearly: If either the Credit risk category is "High" or Affordability category is "Unaffordable," then "Declined", else "Approved". And if we added a second output column to capture the reason for declining, P1 isolates the specific reason in a separate rule, so it could be reported back to the customer. On the other hand, the P2 form (Figure 69) has fewer rules. In this particular case, I would probably lean to P1, but in other circumstances the P2 form is best. There is no absolute right answer.

Which Hit Policy Is Best?

As we have seen, the same decision logic can often be modeled either as a U table, A table, or two different kinds of P table. Which one is best?

On this point, decision table experts do not agree, although there is some consensus around general principles. The first of these is simpler is better, and fewer rules is simpler, thus better. But a second principle says that the rules should make the underlying process logic as easily understood as possible. With regard to hit policy, these principles can pull you in different directions.

Consider the following logic for *Loan eligibility*: if *LTV* is greater than 80% or *Credit score* is below 620 or *Affordability category* is "Unaffordable" then "Ineligible", otherwise "Eligible". Let's compare how this looks with different hit policies.

U	LTV	Credit score	Affordability category	Loan eligibility
	tPercent	tCreditScore [300..850]	tAffordability "Affordable", "Marginal", "Unaffordable"	tEligibility "Eligible", "Ineligible"
1	>80	-	-	"Ineligible"
2	<=80	<620	-	"Ineligible"
3	<=80	>=620	"Unaffordable"	"Ineligible"
4	<=80	>=620	"Marginal","Affordable"	"Eligible"

A	LTV	Credit score	Affordability category	Loan eligibility
	tPercent	tCreditScore [300..850]	tAffordability "Affordable", "Marginal", "Unaffordable"	tEligibility "Eligible", "Ineligible"
1	>80	-	-	"Ineligible"
2	-	<620	-	"Ineligible"
3	-	-	"Unaffordable"	"Ineligible"
4	<=80	>=620	"Marginal","Affordable"	"Eligible"

Figure 70. Equivalent U and A tables

In Figure 70, on the left is the U table, and on the right the corresponding A table. And there is no doubt that the A table here is simpler, easier to create, and better reveals the underlying logic, since each reason for "Ineligible" is isolated in its own rule. Although it's not the case here, often a U table requires more rules than its corresponding A table. And if any of these reasons apply, the A table would be preferred over U. Some decision modeling methodologies, like The Decision Model, simply assume hit policy A.

On the other hand, some decision table experts favor P tables. Figure 71 compares the P table (variant P1, on the left) with the A table for this decision. Here the P table is, as we saw previously, similar to A but slightly simpler, since the else rule is all hyphens. The reasons for "Ineligible" are equally visible and traceable. Here, I would say A and P are equally good choices.

But when decision inputs have a larger number of enumerated values, the P table is often far simpler than A. In the decision depicted in Figure 73 and Figure 73, the P table requires only 7 rules, while the A table requires 14. When P tables require fewer rules, I would generally prefer them over A.

Figure 71. Table P:

P	LTV	Credit score	Affordability category	Loan eligibility
	tPercent	tCreditScore [300..850]	tAffordability "Affordable", "Marginal", "Unaffordable"	tEligibility "Ineligible", "Eligible"
1	>80	-	-	"Ineligible"
2	-	<620	-	"Ineligible"
3	-	-	"Unaffordable"	"Ineligible"
4	-	-	-	"Eligible"

Figure 71. Table A:

A	LTV	Credit score	Affordability category	Loan eligibility
	tPercent	tCreditScore [300..850]	tAffordability "Affordable", "Marginal", "Unaffordable"	tEligibility "Eligible", "Ineligible"
1	>80	-	-	"Ineligible"
2	-	<620	-	"Ineligible"
3	-	-	"Unaffordable"	"Ineligible"
4	<=80	>=620	"Marginal","Affordable"	"Eligible"

Figure 71. Equivalent P1 and A tables

A	Collateral Risk Category	Affordability Category	Credit Risk Category	Qualification
	tCollateralRisk ["Very low", "Low", "Medium", "High"]	tAffordability ["Affordable", "Marginal", "Not affordable"]	tCreditRisk ["A", "B", "C", "D", "E"]	tLoanRecommendation ["Approve", "Decline"]
1		"Affordable"	"A","B","C","D"	"Approve"
2	"Very low"	"Marginal"	"A","B","C"	"Approve"
3			"D"	"Decline"
4		"Affordable"	"A","B","C"	"Approve"
5	"Low"		"D"	"Decline"
6		"Marginal"	"A","B"	"Approve"
7			"C","D"	"Decline"
8		"Affordable"	"A","B"	"Approve"
9	"Medium"		"C","D"	"Decline"
10		"Marginal"	"A"	"Approve"
11			"B","C","D"	"Decline"
12	"High"			"Decline"
13	-	"Not affordable"	-	"Decline"
14	-	-	"E"	"Decline"

Figure 72. A table with many enumerated values

P	Collateral Risk Category	Affordability Category	Credit Risk Category	Qualification
	tCollateralRisk ["Very low", "Low", "Medium", "High"]	tAffordability ["Affordable", "Marginal", "Not affordable"]	tCreditRisk ["A", "B", "C", "D", "E"]	tLoanRecommendation ["Approve", "Decline"]
1	"Very low"	"Affordable"	"A","B","C","D"	"Approve"
2	"Very low"	"Marginal"	"A","B","C"	"Approve"
3	"Low"	"Affordable"	"A","B","C"	"Approve"
4	"Low"	"Marginal"	"A","B"	"Approve"
5	"Medium"	"Affordable"	"A","B"	"Approve"
6	"Medium"	"Marginal"	"A"	"Approve"
7	-	-	-	"Decline"

Figure 73. P table is simpler with many enumerated values

Category with Reasons Pattern

Referring back to Figure 71, even though the P table in principle reveals the reason for ineligibility via the particular rule that matches, technically only the output value "Ineligible" is returned in execution. In order for DMN to return the reason, we need to add a second output column (Figure 74).

P	LTV	Credit score	Affordability category	Loan eligibility	
				Result	Reason
	tPercent	tCreditScore [300..850]	tAffordability "Affordable", "Marginal", "Unaffordable"	tEligibility "Ineligible", "Eligible"	Text
1	>80	-	-	"Ineligible"	"LTV too high"
2	-	<620	-	"Ineligible"	"Credit score too low"
3	-	-	"Unaffordable"	"Ineligible"	"DTI too high"
4	-	-	-	"Eligible"	"Meet LTV, Credit score, DTI requirements"

Figure 74. Category with Reasons pattern

A table with multiple output columns represents a *structured variable* with components. Here we use the component *Result* to hold our original *Loan eligibility* output and add the component *Reason*, a string, to communicate the reason for the decision outcome. Components are referenced with a dot notation, so the result is *Loan eligibility.Result* and the corresponding reason is *Loan eligibility.Reason*. This is sometimes called the *category with reasons pattern*, often useful with both A and P tables.

The Problem with P Tables

There is, however, a problem with P tables, because in some cases they actually obscure the decision logic or make it easy to misinterpret. Consider, for example, the P table shown in Figure 75. The output *Approval Status* could be "Approved", "Declined", or "Referred", meaning sent to a human underwriter. So the question is, when is the *Approval Status* "Referred"?

P	isAffordable	RiskCategory	Approval Status
	Boolean	tRiskCategory "High", "Low", "Medium"	tApprovalStatus "Approved", "Declined", "Referred"
1	true	"Low"	"Approved"
2		"High"	"Declined"
3	-	"Medium"	"Referred"
4	false	-	"Declined"

Figure 75. When is *Approval Status* "Referred"?

You might say, on quick glance, when *RiskCategory* is "Medium", but that's not correct.

The correct answer is when *RiskCategory* is "Medium" and *isAffordable* is true.

Approval Status
tApprovalStatus
"Approved", "Referred", "Declined"

P	inputs		outputs
	isAffordable	**RiskCategory**	**Approval Status**
	Boolean	tRiskCategory "High", "Low", "Medium"	tApprovalStatus "Approved", "Referred", "Declined"
1	true	"Low"	"Approved"
2	true	"High"	"Declined"
3	-	"Medium"	"Referred"
4	false	-	"Declined"

Figure 76. Now when is *Approval Status* "Referred"?

On the other hand, for the P table of Figure 76, it's just when *RiskCategory* is "Medium". The difference is the priority of the "Referred" output value. It is lower than "Declined" in Figure 75 but higher than "Declined" in Figure 76 , so when *RiskCategory* is "Medium" and *isAffordable* is false, Figure 75 gives "Declined" and Figure 76 gives "Referred".

Even though U tables are sometimes harder to construct, they are less ambiguous as to the logic. Figure 77 shows the U table equivalent to Figure 75. In this form it is easy to see the correct answer.

	isAffordable	RiskCategory	Approval Status
U	Boolean	tRiskCategory ["High", "Low", "Medium"]	tApprovalStatus ["Approved", "Referred", "Declined"]
1		"Low"	"Approved"
2	true	"Medium"	"Referred"
3		"High"	"Declined"
4	false	-	"Declined"

Figure 77. U table logic may be clearer than P tables

So you see there is no one-size-fits-all answer to the question which hit policy is best. A has simpler rules than U. P has even simpler rules than A, although you need to watch the order of the output values. In some decisions, P may lead to misinterpretation of the underlying logic, and in such cases, U is better than P. The choice of hit policy really depends on the particular decision logic.

CHAPTER 7

Decision Table Analysis

Although the DMN spec is quite precise and restrictive about certain aspects of decision tables – what you can put in a condition cell for instance – it leaves many aspects of decision table method and style up to the modeler. As we saw in the previous chapter, experts do not always agree on the best hit policy to use in a decision table, but in many other respects they mostly agree on what makes a good decision table. It should be complete, for example, without gaps in the rules. It should be self-consistent, obviously, for any combination of input values. It should be maximally contracted, meaning if multiple rules could be combined into one, they should be so combined.

These properties of a decision table, however, are not required by the DMN spec. Validation of the model against rules of the spec will not report these errors. In Trisotech DMN Modeler, for example, the Validate button simply verifies that the logic has the correct syntax and can be executed.

For that reason, a special feature of this tool called *Decision Table Analysis* checks decision tables for conformance to good decision table style. Clicking the Decision Table Analysis button reports these style errors just like the Validate button reports syntax errors. In this chapter we will look at the various elements of decision table style and their validation using Decision Table Analysis.

Completeness

Decision tables should be *complete*. That means there should be no combination of allowed input values does not match at least one rule. You might say this is obvious, but in fact some decision modeling experts maintain that there is no need for decision tables to be complete, since certain combinations of input values do not occur in real life and the table should not attempt to provide an outcome for them.

Originally DMN provided an indicator that the decision table was intentionally incomplete. That was later eliminated in favor of a *default output entry*, meaning an output value in the case that no rule matches, and you may have seen that in the tool. But default output entry was not specified properly. (It is a unary test, not an expression.) For that reason, I never use the default output value, but instead always make the table complete unless it has hit policy C, Collect, since we don't need to model conditions that do not contribute to the collection.

U	Risk Score	Risk Category
	Number	*tRiskCategory* *["High", "Medium", "Low"]*
1	<10	"Low"
2	(10..30]	"Medium"
3	>30	"High"

Figure 78. An incomplete table

For example, Figure 78 illustrates an incomplete table. There is a gap in the rules when *Risk Score* is 10. To fix it, you could change rule 1 to <=10 or change rule 2 to [10..30]. Decision Table Analysis in the Trisotech tool checks for table completeness and reports gaps in the rules, as shown in Figure 79.

Log Viewer					✕
Severity	Message	Element ▾	Element Type	Page	
☒	Gap: No rule matches for input values [10].	Risk Category	Decision Table	Risk Category	

Figure 79. Decision Table Analysis detects incomplete tables

In simple tables, gaps like this are easy to spot, but in large decision tables, trust me, they are easy to create inadvertently and often hard to see. If Decision Table Analysis reports a gap in a numeric input, pay close attention to the endpoints of the numeric regions. Usually it's something like > should be >=, or parenthesis should be square bracket. With enumerated inputs, fixing a gap typically requires adding a rule for the missing enumeration. If you think that combination could not actually occur, you can always make the output value null. Null is an allowed value for any input type.

Overlaps and Table Consistency

When some combination of input values matches multiple rules in a table, those rules are said to *overlap*. In a U table, rules should not overlap, so overlaps in a U table represent errors.

An Any table, hit policy A, means overlapping rules are allowed if they have the same output value. Overlapping rules with different output values mean the table is *inconsistent*. Again, that is an error. Overlapping rules with different output values require hit policy P, Priority, or C, Collect.

	Risk Score	Risk Category
A	Number	tRiskCategory ["High", "Medium", "Low"]
1	<10	"Low"
2	[10..30]	"Medium"
3	>=30	"High"

Figure 80. An inconsistent table

Severity	Message	Element
☒	Overlap: Rules 2, 3 match with inconsistent output value using input values [30]. Hit policy A requires all matching rules to have same output value.	Risk Category

Figure 81. Decision Table Analysis detects overlaps with inconsistent output

Decision Table Analysis (Figure 81) detects overlaps in U tables and inconsistent A tables. If a U table has overlapping rules with the same output value, simply change the hit policy to A. Inconsistencies are more serious. In Figure 80 you see an inconsistent A table. Decision Table Analysis reports overlap of rules 2 and 3 with Risk Score = 30. We need to fix that, and we can do so by changing rule 3 to >30. Now the table has no overlaps, and the hit policy can be changed to U.

Masked Rules

In a P table, the rules are prioritized by their output value. A rule in a P table is said to be *masked* if its matches are always lower priority than some other matching rule. The most common case of this is an else rule that is not lowest priority. Since the else rule always matches, any lower priority rule is automatically masked.

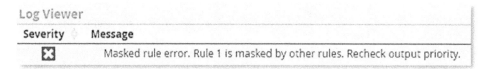

> Order of output values determines their priority. "Declined" must be the last one listed, the lowest priority.

	Age	Risk Category	is Affordable	Approval Sta
P	Number	tRiskCategory ["High", "Medium", "Low"]	Boolean	tApprovalStatus ["Declined", "Approved"]
1	>=18	"Medium","Low"	true	"Approved"
2	.	.	.	"Declined"

	Age	Risk Category	is Affordable	Approval Status
P	Number	tRiskCategory ["High", "Medium", "Low"]	Boolean	tApprovalStatus ["Approved", "Declined"]
1	>=18	"Medium","Low"	true	"Approved"
2	.	.	.	"Declined"

Figure 82. In the table on the left, rule 1 is masked

It's easy to do this by accident. In Figure 82 on the left, rule 1 is always masked by the else rule, rule 2, because "Declined" is not the lowest priority output.

Log Viewer

Severity	Message
☒	Masked rule error. Rule 1 is masked by other rules. Recheck output priority.

Figure 83. Decision Table Analysis detects masked rules

Decision Table Analysis detects masked rules (Figure 83). Fixing masked rules typically means changing the order of the output values in the decision table output column heading. The table on the right is fixed.

Subsumption

Another style rule is that tables should not contain two or more rules that could be combined into one. The technical term for this error is *subsumption*. Combining rules into a single rule is called *contraction*, and it is best practice to contract decision tables as much as possible. Some methodologies like TDM actually require full contraction.

The decision table on the left in Figure 84 is not fully contracted. Decision Table Analysis (Figure 85) says rules 3 and 6 may be combined, and rules 4 and 5 may be combined. Combining 3 and 6 says *Credit Score*>=600 and *PTI* <0.35 gives "Approved". And combining rules 4 and 5 says that *Credit Score*>660 and *PTI*>=0.35 gives "Declined". Even then it's not fully contracted. Running Decision Table Analysis again lets you contract it to 3 rules, as shown on the right in Figure 84.

Incorrect: Table is not contracted

U	CreditScore	PTI	AutoLoanApproval
	Number	Number	tAutoLoanApproval ["Approved", "Declined"]
1	<600	-	"Declined"
2	[600..660]	>=0.35	"Declined"
3		<0.35	"Approved"
4		>=0.38	"Declined"
5	>660	[0.35..0.38)	"Declined"
6		<0.35	"Approved"

Correct: Table is properly contracted

U	CreditScore	PTI	AutoLoanApproval
	Number	Number	tAutoLoanApproval ["Approved", "Declined"]
1	<600	-	"Declined"
2	>=600	>=0.35	"Declined"
3	>=600	<0.35	"Approved"

Figure 84. Subsumption means rules could be combined (not fully contracted)

Log Viewer

Severity	Message	Element	Element Type	Page
❌	Warning: Table is not fully contracted. Combine rules 3, 6.	AutoLoanApproval	Decision Table	AutoLoanApproval
❌	Warning: Table is not fully contracted. Combine rules 4, 5.	AutoLoanApproval	Decision Table	AutoLoanApproval

Figure 85. Decision Table Analysis detects subsumption

Normalization

Some decision table experts have noted that decision tables are in many ways like tables in a database and should adhere to *normalization* principles analogous to those of the Relational Model for databases. These principles define various *normal forms* for the table. Decision table normalization was proposed in the 1990s by Professor Vanthienen[21], and then rediscovered a decade later by von Halle and Goldberg[22]. I don't want to get into the debate about who did what first. The important thing is that the normal forms of the relational model have their analogues in decision table normal forms.

---

[21] Jan Vanthienen, "Rules as Data: Decision Tables and Relational Databases," http://www.brcommunity.com/b516.php

[22] Barbara von Halle and Larry Goldberg, *The Decision Model* (Boca Raton: Taylor and Francis, 2010), http://www.amazon.com/dp/1420082817/

The decision tables discussed by both Vanthienen and TDM predated DMN, and so some of their first normal form violations are already disallowed by DMN, and others may be disallowed by particular DMN tools. The first normal form is the most important. Higher order normal forms are best practices but lower in importance.

First Normal Form

Here are the rules of the First Normal Form as described by von Halle and Goldberg's TDM.

- Column conditions always ANDed, never ORed. This is a rule of the DMN spec.

- Rules are represented as table rows, inputs/outputs as columns. This is one of three formats described in the DMN spec, but it is the most common and the only one currently supported by the Trisotech tool.

- Inputs must be fact types (variables) not expressions. The DMN spec allows input expressions to be any FEEL expression – except where the table is a value expression of a BKM, in which case it must be a simple variable. Currently the Trisotech tool requires input expressions to be simple variables, not expressions.

- Row/column order does not change the result. Effectively this says hit policies F and R violate first normal form, and Decision Table Analysis reports this error. We can always change an F table to P, or an R table to O or C.

- No duplicate rules. This is technically allowed by the DMN spec but is reported by Decision Table Analysis as a first normal form violation.

- Single output column. The table output must be a single fact type, which in TDM is a simple type not a structure. This rule is inappropriate in DMN, where structured variables play an important role. This TDM normalization rule is not used in DMN normalization.

Second Normal Form

The second normal form says that all populated condition cells must be relevant to the outcome. Violations come about when subsumption makes a particular input is irrelevant in a group of rules. Figure 86, an example from von Halle[23], shows the maximum loan-to-value ratio allowed based on the *Mortgage type*, *Number of units*, and the Boolean input *isSecondary*. The table represents a second normal form violation, since rules 1 and 2 represent subsumption, and when you combine them *isSecondary* becomes irrelevant.

Decision Table Analysis (Figure 87) reports the violation. Figure 88, properly contracted, eliminates the error. In the new rule 1, *isSecondary* is hyphen, meaning irrelevant in the rule.

---

[23] http://tdan.com/thedecisionmodeljune2013/16953

U	Mortgage type	Number of units	isSecondary	Max LTV
	Text ["primary residence", "second home"]	Number [1, 2, 3, 4]	Boolean	Number
1	"primary residence"	1	true	0.95
2	"primary residence"	1	false	0.95
3	"primary residence"	2,3,4	true	0.75
4	"primary residence"	2,3,4	false	0.80
5	"second home"	-	true	0.80
6	"second home"	-	false	0.85

Figure 86. Second normal form violation

Log Viewer

Severity	Message
☒	Second normal form violation. Input 3 is irrelevant for rules [1, 2]. Combine those rules for input 3.

Figure 87. Decision Table Analysis detects second normal form violations

U	Mortgage type	Number of units	isSecondary	Max LTV
	Text ["primary residence", "second home"]	Number [1, 2, 3, 4]	Boolean	Number
1	"primary residence"	1	-	0.95
2	"primary residence"	2,3,4	true	0.75
3	"primary residence"	2,3,4	false	0.80
4	"second home"	-	true	0.80
5	"second home"	-	false	0.85

Figure 88. Correction of second normal form violation

Third Normal Form

The third normal form says that all inputs must be *independent*. That means an input column may not represent an implicit conclusion or output of the other inputs. A third normal form violation occurs when the value of one input can always be predicted from the other inputs.

U	Number of units	Mortgage balance	Mortgage eligibility	Mortgage origination date	Mortgage Relief Eligibility
	Number [1, 2, 3, 4]	Number	tMortgageeligibility ["Eligible", "Ineligible"]	Date	tMortgageReliefEligibility ["Eligible", "Ineligible"]
1	1	<700000	"Eligible"	<=date("2013-01-01")	"Eligible"
2	2	<900000	"Eligible"	<=date("2013-01-01")	"Eligible"
3	3	<1000000	"Eligible"	<=date("2013-01-01")	"Eligible"
4	4	<1400000	"Eligible"	<=date("2013-01-01")	"Eligible"
5	1	>=700000	"Ineligible"	<=date("2013-01-01")	"Ineligible"
6	2	>=900000	"Ineligible"	<=date("2013-01-01")	"Ineligible"
7	3	>=1000000	"Ineligible"	<=date("2013-01-01")	"Ineligible"
8	4	>=1400000	"Ineligible"	<=date("2013-01-01")	"Ineligible"
9	-	-	-	>date("2013-01-01")	"Ineligible"

Figure 89. Third normal form violation

The example shown in Figure 89 is also from von Halle, determining eligibility for mortgage relief based on the *Number of units*, the *Mortgage balance*, the *Mortgage eligibility*, and the *Mortgage origination date*. But if you look closely you will see that the *Mortgage eligibility* value, column 3, is always predictable from columns 1 and 2. Thus, it is not really independent, and this table violates the third normal form. Tables with third normal form violations are often incomplete, with many reported gaps. They are rare and require a lot of computation to detect, but Decision Table Analysis does it, as you see here.

Severity	Message
☒	Third normal form violation. Input 3 appears to depend on other inputs.
☒	Gap: No rule matches for input values [1, (1.0E6..1.4E6), "Eligible", <=2013-01-01].
☒	Gap: No rule matches for input values [1, (1.4E6..700000), "Ineligible", <=2013-01-01].
☒	Gap: No rule matches for input values [1, (700000..900000), "Eligible", <=2013-01-01].
☒	Gap: No rule matches for input values [1, (900000..1.0E6), "Eligible", <=2013-01-01].
☒	Gap: No rule matches for input values [1, 1.4E6, "Eligible", <=2013-01-01].
☒	Gap: No rule matches for input values [1, 700000, "Eligible", <=2013-01-01]

Figure 90. Decision Table Analysis detects third normal form violations

The way to fix a third normal form violation is to break out the dependent input into a supporting decision, as you see in Figure 91. *Mortgage Balance Eligibility* is now a supporting decision, using the table shown in Figure 93. Now *Mortgage Relief Eligibility* (Figure 92) is much simpler, and the normal form violations have gone away.

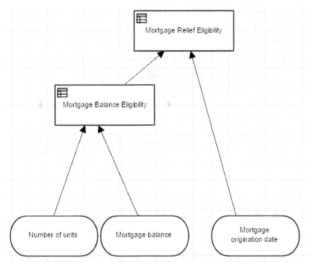

Figure 91. Correcting third normal form violations requires a supporting decision

	Mortgage Balance Eligibility	Mortgage origination date	Mortgage Relief Eligibility
A	tMortgageBalanceEligibility ["Eligible", "Ineligible"]	Date	tMortgageReliefEligibility ["Eligible", "Ineligible"]
1	"Eligible"	<=date("2013-01-01")	"Eligible"
2	"Ineligible"	-	"Ineligible"
3	-	>date("2013-01-01")	"Ineligible"

Figure 92. *Mortgage Relief Eligibility*

U	Number of units	Mortgage balance	Mortgage Balance Eligibility
	Number	Number	tMortgageBalanceEligibility ["Eligible", "Ineligible"]
1	1	<700000	"Eligible"
2	2	<900000	"Eligible"
3	3	<1000000	"Eligible"
4	4	<1400000	"Eligible"
5	1	>=700000	"Ineligible"
6	2	>=900000	"Ineligible"
7	3	>=1000000	"Ineligible"
8	4	>=1400000	"Ineligible"

Figure 93. *Mortgage Balance Eligibility*

CHAPTER 8

Data Modeling and Logic Reuse

What DMN really means by a decision is, given values for certain data, the inputs, what is the value of some other data, the output? The same language, FEEL, DMN uses in its value expressions also defines the particular types of data used in those expressions. Modeling the data you're using, it turns out, is just as important as modeling the logic that goes into decisions.

DMN Data

Every decision, input data, BKM, and decision service in a DRD is represented by a *variable* with the same name as the shape in the DRD. In addition, parameters of BKMs and decision services are variables, as are context entries.

Every variable has a *name*. As we said, variables representing DRD elements have the same name as the shape in the diagram, and this is why DMN variable names may contain spaces and other symbols not normally allowed in other languages.

A variable may be assigned a datatype, or *type*. It's not absolutely required but definitely best practice to explicitly assign every variable to a type. FEEL defines several base types: string, that is, Text; number; Boolean, meaning true or false; and various calendar types: date, time, date and time, days and time duration, and years and months duration.

Values of base types are unconstrained other than being consistent with the type. But it is very common, and also best practice, to add constraints, such as a specific numeric range, or a specific list of enumerated values. Normally this is done by creating a user-defined type, called an *item definition*, specifying those constraints, and assigning the variable to that type.

In addition to constraints on simple types, item definitions are also used to create *structured types*, containing *named components*. In other languages these are sometimes called *business objects*. For example, the type *tBorrower* could have components like *name*, a string; *monthly income*, a number; etc. And item definitions can also specify a *collection* – that is a list, or array – of items of the same type.

Most variables also have a *value expression*, a formula or set of rules that determines their value, also called the *decision logic*. A few variables, such as input data and BKM parameters, have no value expression. They simply receive a value when they are executed.

It is important to keep in mind the distinction between a *value*, such as what is entered and returned in test execution, and a *value expression*, the text formula used in the decision logic. For example, "OK" is a literal expression that returns the string value OK. 1+1 is a literal expression that returns the number value 2.

Data in Decision Tables

In a decision table, each input and output should have a specified type. In Figure 94 we see they have just been assigned to base types, so, for example, any text would be a valid input entry for *Affordability category*.

U	Affordability category	Credit score	Loan approval
	Text	Number	Text
1	"Affordable"	>680	"Likely approved"
2	"Affordable"	[620..680]	"Possibly approved"
3	"Affordable"	<620	"Likely disapproved"
4	"Marginal"	>720	"Likely approved"
5	"Marginal"	[680..720]	"Possibly approved"
6	"Marginal"	<680	"Likely disapproved"
7	"Unaffordable"	-	"Likely disapproved"

Figure 94. Unconstrained inputs and outputs

But that's not really right, since our logic only considers specific enumerated values. In the input column heading we can click, for example, the base type Text and define certain allowed values, as you see in Figure 95: "Affordable", "Marginal", "Unaffordable" for *Affordability Category*, or the numeric range 300-850 inclusive for *Credit score*. When you do it this way, any other values for those inputs are disallowed in the decision table.

	Affordability category	Credit score	Loan approval
U	Text "Affordable", "Marginal", "Unaffordable"	Number [300..850)	Text
1	"Affordable"	>680	"Likely approved"
2	"Affordable"	[620..680]	"Possibly approved"
3	"Affordable"	<620	"Likely disapproved"
4	"Marginal"	>720	"Likely approved"
5	"Marginal"	[680..720]	"Possibly approved"
6	"Marginal"	<680	"Likely disapproved"
7	"Unaffordable"	-	"Likely disapproved"

Figure 95. Input and output values constrained in this decision table

But when you do it that way, the constraints apply only to that decision table. More often you want to say that this variable, wherever its used in this model, always has those constraints. And the way to do that is to create a *named type* for it, an *item definition*. This helps to document the decision logic, standardize the business vocabulary, and promote reuse… so it's generally best practice. The Trisotech tool makes it easy to create an item definition. When you create constraints, the dialog has a button *Create Type*. If you click it, the tool creates a named type for you, with a default name – you can change it – and saves it in the model.

Figure 96 is the same decision table with named types assigned to the inputs and output. This is the best way to do it.

U	Affordability category	Credit score	Loan approval
	tAffordabilitycategory "Affordable", "Marginal", "Unaffordable"	tCreditscore [300..850)	tLoanapproval "Likely approved", "Possibly approved", "Likely disapproved"
1	"Affordable"	>680	"Likely approved"
2	"Affordable"	[620..680]	"Possibly approved"
3	"Affordable"	<620	"Likely disapproved"
4	"Marginal"	>720	"Likely approved"
5	"Marginal"	[680..720]	"Possibly approved"
6	"Marginal"	<680	"Likely disapproved"
7	"Unaffordable"	-	"Likely disapproved"

Figure 96. Input and output value constraints defined by named types

Structured Types and Collections

Often several data elements can be considered *attributes* of some larger object. You could make them all separate variables linked by some naming convention, but in DMN it's better to make them *components of a structured type*. For example, the borrower has a name, an ID, Age, monthly income, and many other attributes. So it's best to define a type *tBorrower* with each of these elements defined as a *component* (Figure 97). Each component has a name and a type. In FEEL, individual components are referenced using a dot notation, such as *Borrower.name*.

Suppose there are two borrowers on the loan, *Borrower1* and *Borrower2*. They don't have separate types; both are assigned to *tBorrower*, so for example, the combined monthly income is *Borrower1.monthly income + Borrower2.monthly income*.

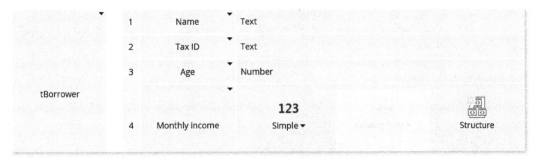

1	Name	Text
2	Tax ID	Text
3	Age	Number
tBorrower		
		123
4	Monthly Income	Simple ▼

Structure

Figure 97. Defining a structured type in Trisotech Decision Modeler

A type also may be specified as a *collection*, a list or array of items of the same type. A table is a collection of a structured type. Each column in the table is a *component* of the structure, and each row is an *item* in the collection. In the Trisotech tool, a marker with three vertical bars signifies the type is a collection. For example, *tBorrowers* (Figure 98) is a table of borrowers, each row defined by the *tBorrower* structure.

tBorrowers
III   tBorrower »

Figure 98. A collection type

In the Trisotech tool, the Datatype button on the DMN ribbon lists all the item definitions in the model (Figure 99). You can Add a new type or click the pencil to edit an existing type.

Figure 99. Item definition list in Trisotech Decision Modeler

Data Standardization and Reuse

All this naming and typing maybe seems like a lot of extra work. You want to get on to defining the decision logic. But one thing that decision management experts have preached for decades – long before DMN came on the scene – is that the key to success is *standardizing the business vocabulary*. That means not only using *named types* and documenting and reusing those types as much as possible, but standardizing the *variables* commonly used in the business – their names and types – and documenting their meaning and usage in a *data dictionary* or *business glossary* shared across the organization.

Business Glossary

The DMN standard does not provide any requirements or even guidance for what such a dictionary or glossary should provide or look like. Every tool is different. So here is how it works in the Trisotech DMN Modeler.

In every decision, input data, BKM, or decision service, if you right click Details you can enter a detailed description, along with comments and links, defining its associated variable. It is important to take the time to do this, as *this becomes the variable's entry in the business glossary*. The Details panel also shows the assigned datatype and where the variable is used. Datatypes currently do not have equivalent documentation, just the simple naming of base type and constraints. If that is insufficient – which is sometimes the case – you need to explain that in the details of a variable based on the type.

On the DRD page of the model is a string of icons at the top right. The first one, outlined with a box in Figure 100, opens the *Scope panel*, which lists all the variables and knowledge sources accessible in the *current model*, including those imported from other models. If you click the variable name, the Details panel for that variable opens, where you see the description, type, where used, links to further documentation, etc. (Figure 101). This panel acts as the business glossary for the current model.

The next icon, the book, opens the *Dictionary panel*, showing the variables defined in the *current repository* or *Place* (Figure 102). It presents a hierarchy of folders, models, and variables, with description from the Details panel. This can be viewed as the business glossary at the Place level, although it does not enforce a single definition for variables and types used everywhere in the Place.

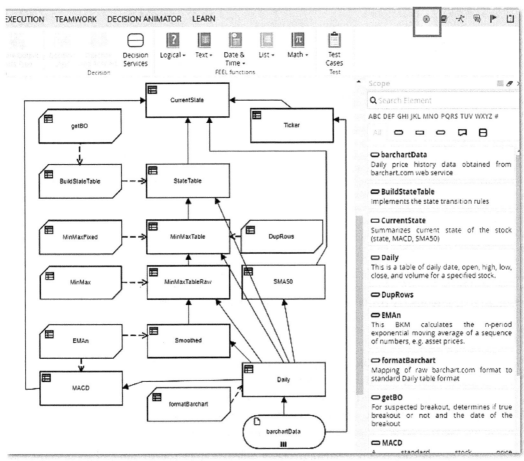

Figure 100. Scope panel is glossary of elements in scope of the current model

Figure 101. Element details provides data definition, where-used, and comments

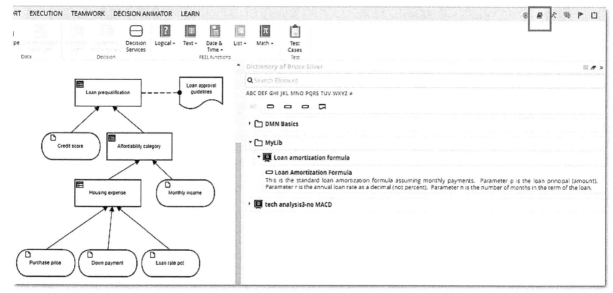

Figure 102. Dictionary panel is glossary of the current repository

Model Libraries

To encourage reuse of variables and types, it is a good idea to store the models that define them in special folders shared with other users. These folders act as *libraries,* from which you or other modelers can copy or import not only the variable name and type but their decision logic. Commonly reused fragments of decision logic are normally saved in these libraries as BKMs or decision services, and we'll see how to do that, and how to reuse these items created by others.

Variables and types are stored at the model level. Each model has a unique *namespace* – typically a long, impossible-to-remember URL – allowing uniqueness of names to be maintained at that level. When you *import* a model into another model, you assign it an *import prefix,* a shorter easier-to-remember string that just must be unique in the importing model. This prevents accidental name collisions when you reuse elements imported from a model library.

Access control to shared libraries is always important. In the Trisotech environment, access is shared at the repository or Place level. Within a Place you can create folders containing multiple models. The tool lets you search for objects across Places, or within a Place.

Model Import

In the Trisotech DMN Modeler, if you drag an element from the Dictionary panel onto your DRD, you are *importing* that element into your model (Figure 103). Here, for example, when we drag the BKM *Loan Amortization Formula* from the *MyLib* folder in the current Place and drop it in the DRD, it shows up with a *lock icon,* meaning it is a *reference* to an imported definition. We cannot modify it in the current model. To change it you need to edit the original source model. Note that elements dragged from the Places panel are not imported and do not work this way. That just creates an editable copy in your current model.

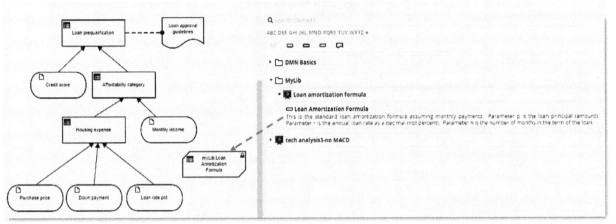

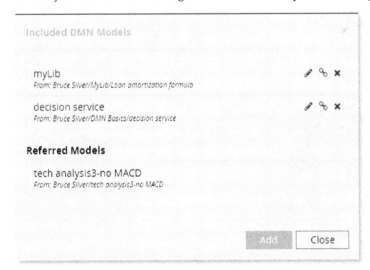

Figure 103. Drag from Dictionary panel creates a reference to the original element

The imported BKM label includes a prefix followed by a dot and then the original name. The prefix prevents name conflicts between imported names and names currently defined in the model. The tool defaults the prefix to the original model name, here *Loan amortization formula*, but lets you edit it to something more suitable for a prefix. I changed it to *myLib*.

Figure 104. Include button imports all elements of a selected model, with user-defined prefix

We can also import models stored anywhere in the workspace, not only in the current Place, with the *Include* button on the DMN ribbon. This lets you navigate to any Place you have access to in the workspace and select a model to import. You can see all the models imported in your current model, as well as those that they in turn have imported, called *Referred* (Figure 104).

Import – whether via the Include button or dragging from the Dictionary panel – works at the *model level*. You import *all* elements and types from that model, not just one. Once you import a model, it shows up in the Scope panel with its assigned prefix and can be dragged onto the DRD from there (Figure 105).

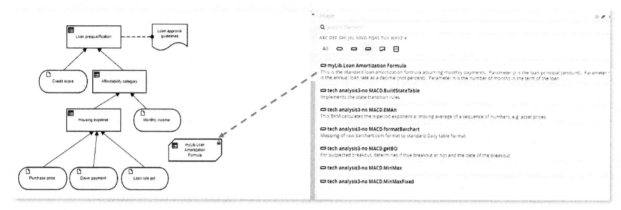

Figure 105. Imported models appear in the Scope panel with prefix

CHAPTER 9

Classification Patterns

Classification is the most basic pattern in decision modeling. It means assigning a combination of input values to some enumerated output value, such as a category, level, rating, or other output determination. Most decision tables do no more than this. We also use classification to convert continuous values – such as numbers or dates – to enumerated values.

In DMN, classification typically uses a *decision table*, in which the output column has enumerated values, such as a *Risk Category* decision with allowed values "High", "Medium", or "Low". In a decision table, the classification is based on *decision rules* on each input. If each input entry in the rule is true, the rule matches and the output classification is selected, subject to the hit policy, as we've discussed.

These rules come from two types of sources. One is from regulations, organization policies, embedded application logic, or external requirements. They are effectively *given to us*. Our job is to translate them into a form that a decision table can execute. We've mostly been talking about this type of source.

But others are just our best attempt to predict an outcome. For example, what is the risk that this claim is fraudulent, or that we may lose this customer? No one is going to give us the rules for these predictions. In the best case, they are based on *analytical models* that look at historical data – often our own data collected from experience – and predict, for example, whether a claim is likely valid or fraudulent, or whether this customer is at high or low risk of leaving.

Classification and Machine Learning

Today it is common to adopt the language of *data science* to discuss the latter type of classification as *data mining*. It is often implemented via *machine learning*, in which we *train* a system by feeding it many cases with known outcome, and then ask it to *predict* the outcome for some new instances. In addition to this supervised machine learning, you may also hear about unsupervised machine learning, also called deep learning, used to classify unstructured data such as natural language in a chatbot, or an image in a face recognition system.

The type of machine learning relevant to DMN is the supervised or trained type. There are a wide variety of machine learning algorithms that can be applied to data for classification. Some but not all of them can be translated into decision logic implemented in DMN. For example, algorithms creating *decision trees* or based on *logistic regression* can be expressed as DMN decision tables. We're very interested in those, because they make the logic of the machine learning algorithm transparent, understandable to human beings. In this sense, DMN is beginning to play an important role in business as "explainable AI." Other machine learning algorithms modeled using the Predictive Modeling Markup Language (PMML) can be invoked by DMN as BKMs and decision services.[24]

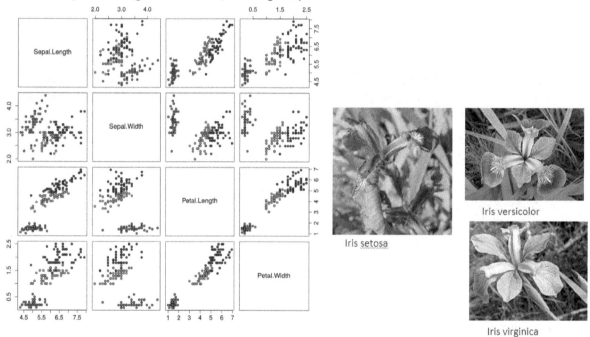

Figure 106. Machine learning-generated classifications of iris types by petal and sepal length and width

A big part of what data scientists do in developing these machine learning models is called "feature engineering", extracting details of the raw Big Data into "features" important to the classification. In DMN we do something like this as well, using *supporting decisions* in the DRD to convert low-level input data into *features* that can be processed by our top-level decision. As

---

[24] https://en.wikipedia.org/wiki/Predictive_Model_Markup_Language

discussed in depth in the *DMN Cookbook*,[25] DMN's expression language FEEL supports a rich set of functions and operators that support this type of feature engineering in decision models.

Normalizing Raw Data

Machine learning algorithms are beyond the scope of this book. Instead we're going to focus on simple classification logic. One use we mentioned was converting continuous variables, such as numbers, to enumerated categories.

One benefit of doing that is that it lets us put disparate sources of raw numeric data on a common footing for further decision logic. You could call this the most basic form of feature engineering. For example, American students applying to college take one of two aptitude tests, the SAT or the ACT. They test more or less the same thing, but their scoring is completely different. Also, the scores in each percentile change from year to year. Suppose you want to use these scores in your college admission decision. Classifying the scores based on categories keyed to percentiles lets you do it.

---

[25] Bruce Silver and Edson Tirelli, *DMN Cookbook* (Altadena, Cody-Cassidy Press, 2018), https://www.amazon.com/dp/0982368186

P	SAT Score	ACT Score	Aptitude Test Category
	Number	Number	tAptitudeCategory "Outstanding", "Excellent", "Very Good", "Good", "Fair", "Ineligible"
1	>=1475	-	"Outstanding"
2	[1400..1475)	-	"Excellent"
3	[1325..1400)	-	"Very Good"
4	[1200..1325)	-	"Good"
5	[1055..1200)	-	"Fair"
6	<1055	-	"Ineligible"
7	-	>=34	"Outstanding"
8	-	[31..34)	"Excellent"
9	-	[29..31)	"Very Good"
10	-	[24..29)	"Good"
11	-	[20..24)	"Fair"
12	-	<20	"Ineligible"

Figure 107. Classification to normalize raw values

In Figure 107, for example, we've defined six categories and a decision table assigning ranges of test scores to each category. There is the small chance that a student has taken both SAT and ACT, and in this case I've elected to use a P table that – given the priority order of the output values – selects the higher category in that case.

Supporting Decisions as Classifications

Supporting decisions in the DRD are often themselves classifications. Modeling complex decision logic as a hierarchy of classification decisions has the benefit of simplifying the decision logic. Instead of a single decision with many inputs and rules, we have multiple decisions each with a smaller number of inputs and rules. This makes the overall logic easier to understand and to maintain.

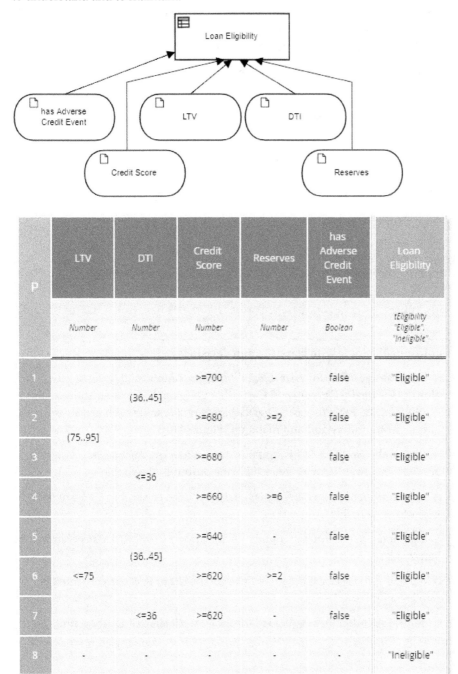

P	LTV	DTI	Credit Score	Reserves	has Adverse Credit Event	Loan Eligibility
	Number	Number	Number	Number	Boolean	tEligibility "Eligible", "Ineligible"
1	(75..95]	(36..45]	>=700	-	false	"Eligible"
2	(75..95]	(36..45]	>=680	>=2	false	"Eligible"
3	(75..95]	<=36	>=680	-	false	"Eligible"
4	(75..95]	<=36	>=660	>=6	false	"Eligible"
5	<=75	(36..45]	>=640	-	false	"Eligible"
6	<=75	(36..45]	>=620	>=2	false	"Eligible"
7	<=75	<=36	>=620	-	false	"Eligible"
8	-	-	-	-	-	"Ineligible"

Figure 108. FNMA *Loan Eligibility* based on raw data

Figure 108 provides an example. This decision table represents eligibility of a mortgage loan for purchase by Fannie Mae, an organization that securitizes loans. The logic here is a single table with 5 inputs, all raw numeric input data, and 8 rules. While it accurately reflects FNMA's requirements for a particular year, we can make it simpler, more understandable, and more maintainable by factoring it into simpler supporting decisions.

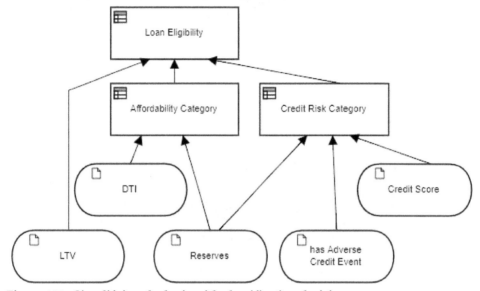

Figure 109. Simplifying the logic with classification decisions

In Figure 109 we've made the DRD for *Loan Eligibility* more complicated, inserting two new supporting decisions, *Affordability Category* and *Credit Risk Category*, both classifications. But in so doing, we've simplified the logic for *Loan Eligibility*. It's now a table with just three inputs and 5 rules that are easier to understand and maintain (Figure 110).

- If the loan-to-value ratio *LTV* is greater than 95% or *Affordability Category* is "Unaffordable" or *Credit Risk Category* is "E", the output is "Ineligible".

- If *LTV* is high and *Affordability Category* is "Marginal", the *Credit Risk Category* must be "A" in order to be "Eligible".

- If *LTV* is high and *Affordability Category* is "Affordable", *Credit Risk Category* must be "B" or better to be "Eligible".

- If *LTV* is low and *Affordability Category* is "Marginal", *Credit Risk Category* must be "C" or better to be "Eligible".

- If *LTV* is low and *Affordability Category* is "Affordable", *Credit Risk Category* must be "D: or better to be "Eligible".

	LTV	Affordability Category	Credit Risk Category	Loan Eligibility
P	Number	tAffordabilityCategory "Affordable", "Marginal", "Unaffordable"	tCreditRiskCategory "A", "B", "C", "D", "E"	tEligibility "Eligible", "Ineligible"
1	(75..95]	"Affordable", "Marginal"	"A"	"Eligible"
2		"Affordable"	"A","B"	"Eligible"
3	<=75	"Affordable", "Marginal""	"A","B","C"	"Eligible"
4		"Affordable"	"A","B","C","D"	"Eligible"
5	-	-	-	"Ineligible"

Figure 110. *Loan Eligibility* **using classified inputs**

These three features – *LTV, Affordability,* and *Credit Risk* – have clear and distinct meaning and make the *Loan Eligibility* logic simpler and more understandable. Moreover, the logic for *Loan Eligibility* should be stable through annual changes in FNMA requirements, which just affect the credit score and DTI limits that determine *Affordability Category* and *Credit Risk Category.*

Affordability Category uses the borrower's debt to income ratio *DTI* and liquid asset *Reserves* to classify loan affordability as "Affordable", "Marginal", or "Unaffordable" (Figure 111). *Credit Risk Category* uses the borrower's *Credit score* in combination with *Reserves* to classify into five levels, "A," "B", "C," "D", and "E", "A" being the best risk and "E" the worst (Figure 112). If the borrower's credit report shows a past *Adverse Credit Event* such as bankruptcy, *Credit Risk Category* is automatically "E".

U	DTI	Reserves	Affordability Category
	Number	Number	tAffordabilityCategory "Affordable", "Marginal", "Unaffordable"
1	>45	-	"Unaffordable"
2	(36..45]	<2	"Marginal"
3	(36..45]	>=2	"Affordable"
4	<=36	-	"Affordable"

Figure 111. *Affordability Category* classification

U	Credit Score	Reserves	has Adverse Credit Event	Credit Risk Category
	Number	Number	Boolean	tCreditRiskCategory "A", "B", "C", "D", "E"
1	>700	-	false	"A"
2	[680..700)	-	false	"B"
3	[660..680)	>=6	false	"B"
4	[660..680)	<6	false	"C"
5	[640..660)	-	false	"C"
6	[620..640)	-	false	"D"
7	<620	-	false	"E"
8	-	-	true	"E"

Figure 112. *Credit Risk Category* classification

Combining Ordered Classifications

In the previous example, the *Credit Risk Category* decision defines a list of category values "A" through "E" with a distinct order, best to worst. Often in DMN a decision table must combine inputs representing such *ordered classifications* to determine a result, such as "Eligible" vs "Ineligible". This is a common decision table pattern.

Let's assume the rules take the following form:

```
if conditionA and conditionB and ConditionC then "Eligible" else "Ineligible"
```

where *conditionA* means a Boolean condition on input A. And here let's say A, B, and C are all ordered classifications: A could be either "Good" or "Bad"; B could be "Good", "Fair", or "Bad"; and C could be "Best", "Good", "Fair", or "Bad". The rules might be something like this:

- "Eligible" if A and B are both "Good" and C is "Fair" or better.

- "Eligible" if A is "Good", B is "Fair", and C is "Good" or better.

- "Ineligible" if A is "Good" and both B and C are "Fair".

- "Ineligible" if any of A, B, or C is "Bad".

The U table for this, with 6 rules, is shown in Figure 113 on the left. We can make a simpler P table with only 4 rules, shown on the right, that more clearly reveals the logic.

	A	B	C	Eligibility
U	tA "Good", "Bad"	tB "Good", "Fair", "Bad"	tC "Best", "Good", "Fair", "Bad"	tEligibility "Eligible", "Ineligible"
1	"Good"	"Good"	"Best", "Good", "Fair"	"Eligible"
2	"Good"	"Fair"	"Best", "Good"	"Eligible"
3	"Good"	"Fair"	"Fair"	"Ineligible"
4	"Good"	"Good", "Fair"	"Bad"	"Ineligible"
5	"Good"	"Bad"	-	"Ineligible"
6	"Bad"	-	-	"Ineligible"

	A	B	C	Eligibility
P	tA "Good", "Bad"	tB "Good", "Fair", "Bad"	tC "Best", "Good", "Fair", "Bad"	tEligibility "Eligible", "Ineligible"
1		"Good"	"Best", "Good", "Fair"	"Eligible"
2	"Good"	"Fair"	"Best", "Good"	"Eligible"
3			"Fair"	"Ineligible"
4	.	.	.	"Ineligible"

Figure 113. Combining ordered classifications

Figure 110 is the same pattern applied to what we have been discussing, *Loan Eligibility*. Learning to recognize and use patterns like these is helpful to becoming a proficient decision modeler.

Category-Score Pattern

Sometimes the appropriate weight applied to each input in a classification rules is not so simply specified. Various factors may contribute to the overall decision, but individually no one is decisive. The *category-score pattern* in DMN addresses this by assigning *scores* to various features, or input combinations, summing them to compute a total score, and classifying the total score. The score for an individual feature acts as its *weight* in the overall classification. This is analogous to the machine learning technique called *logistic regression*, which finds the optimum list of features and their score or weight. Here we will just guess at the proper weights.

The category score pattern uses two decision tables. In the *score decision*, each rule assigns a weight or score to some combination of input values. We expect multiple rules to match, so the score decision has the hit policy C+, meaning collect and sum, adding up the scores of the rules that match to give a total score. The *category decision* takes the score decision as its input and classifies the score into categories based on "cuts" in the score.

For example, in lending decisions, in addition to the amount of borrower income, the underwriter must determine the stability and continuity of that income. He could for example attach an *Income Risk Category* to the number based on whether the income is from salary, self-employment, or incentive compensation, whether the income has been continuous and increasing or stable over a period of years, etc. That's what we have in Figure 114.

C+	Employment type	Two-year continuous income	Income trend	Incentive percent	Rental royalty investment percent	Income Risk Score
	Text "Regular", "Self-employed", "Retired", "Unemployed"	Boolean	Text "Increasing", "Stable", "Decreasing"	Number	Number	Number
1	"Retired","Unemployed"	-	-	-	-	20
2	"Regular","Self-employed"	false	"Stable", "Decreasing"	-	-	20
3	"Self-employed"	true	"Stable"	-	-	5
4	"Self-employed"	true	"Decreasing"	-	-	20
5	"Regular"	true	"Decreasing"	-	-	10
6	"Regular"	true	-	>25	-	5
7	"Regular"	true	-	>50	-	15
8	-	-	-	-	>25	10
9	-	-	-	-	>50	20

Figure 114. The score decision in category-score pattern

	Income Risk Score	Income Risk Category
U		
	Number	tRiskCategory "Low", "Moderate", "High"
1	>=35	"High"
2	[10..35)	"Moderate"
3	<10	"Low"

Figure 115. Category decision in category-score pattern

The score decision provides a weight or score for each combination of input values. In this case, higher score means higher risk. C+ means add up those scores, and then the category decision (Figure 115) classifies the result: *Income Risk Category* is "High" if the score is 35 or higher, "Moderate" from 10 to 34, and "Low" if under 10.

CHAPTER 10

Decision Services

Technically a *decision service* is a unit of decision logic execution. A model could be executed all at once – we've seen that with Trisotech's *Publish to Cloud Execution* button – or we can define within a model a specific fragment that is executed as a unit. Because DMN decision models do not take actions – they just return data values – DMN decision services are always *stateless*. That's geek-speak for saying they are easily scalable in production and compatible with modern IT architectures like microservices.

Prior to DMN 1.2, a decision service could be invoked, that is, executed, only by an external client app or process, but DMN 1.2 added the ability to invoke a service by a decision or BKM. In the latter case, a decision service acts much like a BKM. There are a few differences, as you see in this table:

BKM	Decision Service
Invoked by decision or another BKM	Invoked by decision, BKM, or external client
Defined as a single value expression (possibly a context)	Defined as a sub-DRD
... may have multiple components	... may have multiple output decisions
Invoked as a single DRG element	Invoked as a single DRG element

Figure 116. BKM vs Decision Service

A BKM can only be invoked by a decision or another BKM, but in addition to those a decision service can be invoked by an external client, such as an app or business process. While a BKM is always a single element in the DRD, with a single value expression – you could use a *context* to fit complex logic into it, but it's always a single node – a decision service is more flexible. You model it as a DRD, and it can have more than one output decision.

In addition to publishing the model as a whole as a service, we're going to talk about three other usage patterns:

1. In a decision model meant to be executed in multiple steps, we can use decision services to illustrate those steps.

2. Commonly used logic fragments can be imported from model libraries and reused in your decision model.

3. You can delegate the implementation of a decision in your DRD to someone else, in the form of a decision service your decision invokes.

Visualize Execution Steps

In the DMN spec there is an example of a Lending decision that is executed in multiple steps. From the DRD (Figure 117) you would have no idea it takes three steps, or what is in each step. The spec suggests that information is provided by a separate process model, but that is not entirely satisfactory. It really should be in the DRD itself, and decision services provide a way to do that.

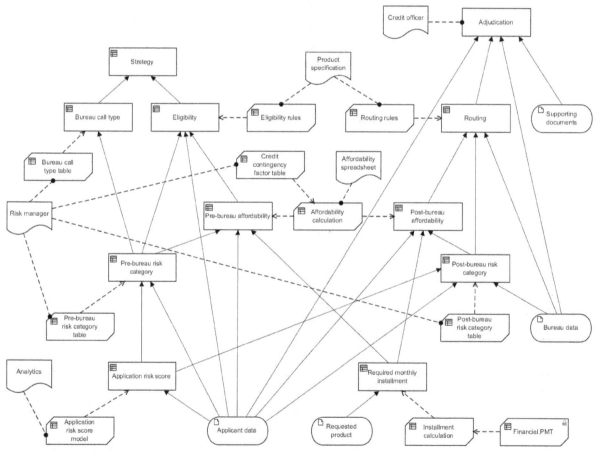

Figure 117. Lending decision example from DMN spec

This example was the origin of decision services in DMN, which defined a new shape, a rounded rectangle with a thick border enclosing the decisions comprising the service. This rounded rectangle is an overlay on the DRD, so a single decision could belong to more than one service. Information requirements crossing into the decision service define its parameters, that is, its inputs. A line bisecting the rounded rectangle, separates output decisions, which return their value on execution, from other so-called encapsulated decisions, which do not.

Wizard-Based Service Definition

That sounds good, but in practice it doesn't always work, especially when some decisions, like *Application Risk Score* and *Required Monthly Installment*, are members of two different services (Figure 118). Defining the service boundary as a rounded rectangle makes drawing the DRD just too hard. A freeform polygon, like you see here, would make more sense. Here you see the *Strategy* service has two output decisions, and the *Routing* service only one.

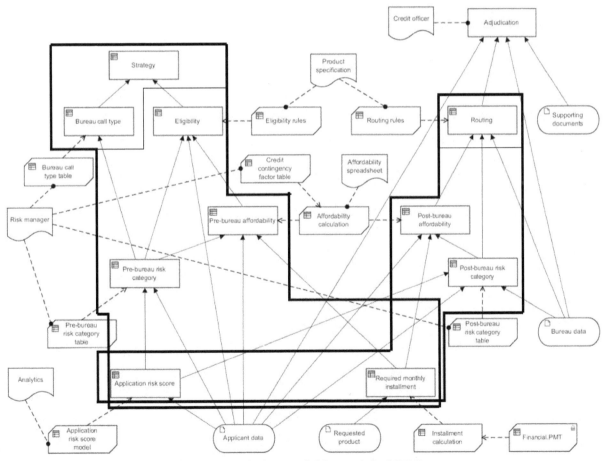

Figure 118. Decision service boundaries overlaid on original DRD

To get around that problem, the Trisotech tool provides a wizard, the *Decision Services* button on the DMN ribbon, which lets you select from the DRD the output decisions and encapsulated decisions, and the wizard figures out the inputs (Figure 119).

Figure 119. Trisotech Decision Service wizard as alternative selection of service elements

When you create a service using the wizard, its definition is automatically created on its own DRD page of the model, where the rounded rectangle notation works well. Note that a single decision model may have more than one DRD page, and shapes on two different pages can reference the same semantic element.

DRD 1   DRD 2

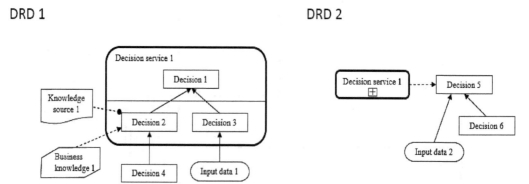

Figure 120. Expanded and contracted representations of decision service notation

Figure 120 illustrates the notation. In DMN 1.2, the decision service shape was given two forms: *expanded*, as in DRD1 on the left, and *collapsed* – a single node with a plus sign – as in DRD2 on the right. We use the expanded shape to *define the service*. The shape encloses one or more decision nodes in the DRD. Decisions above the line are exposed as *outputs*; those below the line, called *encapsulated decisions*, are used in the logic but their output values are not returned.

Information requirements crossing into the service define the *parameters* of the service, the inputs. On the left they are called *Decision 4* and *Input data 1*. Those are the parameter names; it doesn't matter that in the definition view one is a decision and the other is input data; in the service they are just parameters.

The collapsed shape on the right is used to *invoke the service* via a knowledge requirement, like a BKM. Here you see *Decision 5* invokes *Decision service 1*. Remember invocation simply means passing values to its parameters, which here are called *Decision 4* and *Input data 1*. So the invocation expression maps *Decision 5*'s inputs, *Decision 6* and *Input data 2*, to those parameters.

Importing Services as Reusable Logic

Decision services provide a way to reuse decision logic fragments created by others by importing them as services and invoking them from your decisions. In this respect, decision services act like BKMs, except they are defined as DRDs rather than single value expressions.

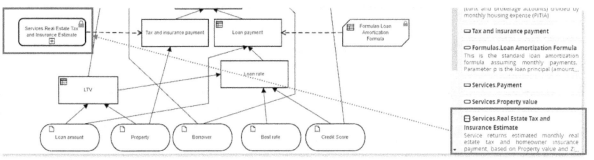

Figure 121. Inserting imported decision service

Figure 121 is a fragment of a more fully elaborated version of a mortgage-related decision similar to the DRD of Figure 51. In the simpler version, the *Tax and insurance payment* formula used an average rate independent of the property location. In a more realistic scenario, those rates would be looked up from a large table of real estate tax rates and homeowner insurance rates, by ZIP code.

In a lender organization, this is a commonly used function, already implemented as a decision service that returns the monthly tax and insurance payment for a property, given *Property.Value* and *Property.Location.PostalCode*. That service is stored in a model library for reuse. The modeler doesn't need to know how to code the service, just how to import and use it. And that's what we have in Figure 121.

As described previously, the modeler uses the *Include* button to navigate to the *Services* folder, a library of shared decision services, and import the model *Real Estate Tax and Insurance Estimate*. The modeler selects the prefix *Services* for this import, so in the Scope panel it is listed as *Services.Real Estate Tax and Insurance Estimate*. The service details specify its inputs as *Property value*, a number, and *ZIP code*, which is text.

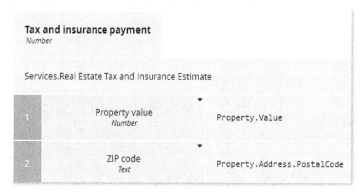

Tax and insurance payment
Number

Services.Real Estate Tax and Insurance Estimate

| 1 | Property value *Number* | Property.Value |
| 2 | ZIP code *Text* | Property.Address.PostalCode |

Figure 122. Boxed invocation of imported decision service

All the modeler needs to do is invoke it. As seen from the boxed invocation (Figure 122), this is very simple. Note that while the prefix *Services* is used to name the invoked service, it is not used in the parameter names.

Services as Delegated Implementation

Decision services have a second important usage pattern. It looks similar to the previous one, but its motivation is not about standardization and reuse. We know that a complete DRD, with datatypes specified for all the nodes, provides a detailed outline of the overall decision logic even if we have not defined the logic of the nodes. For some decisions in the DRD, we may not even know how to model that logic. That's ok, since we can *delegate the implementation* to a more technical modeler or subject matter expert. Since that logic is specific to our decision model, it's typically not saved off to some external library, but added right in our model.

So here we're going to pretend to be the person tasked with implementing the decision logic, and we're going to see how to create the decision service ourselves. In mortgage lending, the actual loan rate offered to a borrower is usually not the current "best rate" published in the newspaper. That's available only to the lowest risk applicants, with low loan-to-value ratio and very high credit scores. For everyone else, the loan rate offered is slightly higher.

That is because in order to securitize the loan, FNMA charges the lender a risk premium called *Loan Level Price Adjustment* (LLPA), a percentage of the loan amount based on the borrower's credit score and the loan to value ratio. The lender typically passes on this adjustment to the borrower by increasing the loan rate, around one eighth of a percent per percent of LLPA. We're going to model the logic for the *Adjusted loan rate* as a decision service.

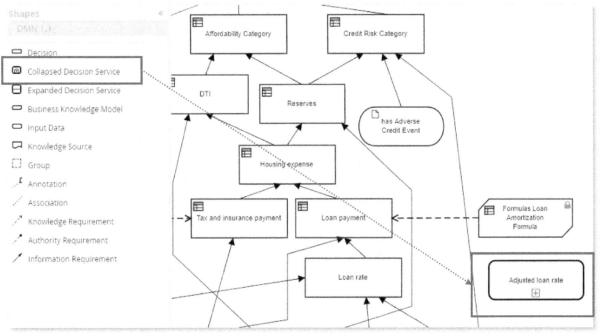

Figure 123. Inserting decision service from Shapes panel

In Figure 123 we have inserted a collapsed decision service shape into the DRD, *Adjusted loan rate*, datatype *tPercent*, meaning a number expressed as a percent. Clicking the + sign at the bottom center of the service opens up a new DRD page in the model where we define the service (Figure 124).

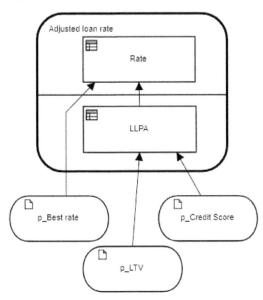

Figure 124. Decision service definition in its own DRD

This DRD contains only the service definition. Decisions placed above the line are exposed as outputs of the decision; those below the line are called encapsulated, and their output values are not visible on execution. Input data drawn outside the service boundary and connected to service components by information requirements define its input parameters. If the service invokes any BKMs or other services, they are also drawn outside the service boundary and connected by knowledge requirements.

In the *Adjusted loan rate* service, the combination of loan-to-value and credit score determine the *Loan Level Price Adjustment*, using a formula posted on the FNMA website.[26] Inside the service boundary, we add an output decision *Rate*, type *tPercent*, and an encapsulated decision *LLPA*, also type *tPercent*. The service parameters are represented by three input data elements, *p_Best rate*, type *tPercent*, with an information requirement directly to *Rate*, *p_Credit Score*, type *tCreditScore*, with an information requirement to *LLPA*, and *p_LTV*, type *tPercent*, connected to *LLPA* (Figure 124).

These input data are just the names of the parameters of the service. But unlike BKM parameters, they are not exclusively "owned" by the service. Since a decision service is an overlay on model elements that could be used elsewhere, I like to give them names different from the names of other elements in our model, which is why I have prefixed them with *p_*. It's not absolutely necessary, but I've found it cleaner to make sure that the names of decision service parameters are distinguished from the names of other model variables.

Representative Credit Score	LTV Range							
	Applicable for all mortgages with terms greater than 15 years							
	≤ 60.00%	60.01 – 70.00%	70.01 – 75.00%	75.01 – 80.00%	80.01 – 85.00%	85.01 – 90.00%	90.01 – 95.00%	95.01 – 97.00%
≥ 740	0.000%	0.250%	0.250%	0.500%	0.250%	0.250%	0.250%	0.750%
720 – 739	0.000%	0.250%	0.500%	0.750%	0.500%	0.500%	0.500%	1.000%
700 – 719	0.000%	0.500%	1.000%	1.250%	1.000%	1.000%	1.000%	1.500%
680 – 699	0.000%	0.500%	1.250%	1.750%	1.500%	1.250%	1.250%	1.500%
660 – 679	0.000%	1.000%	2.250%	2.750%	2.750%	2.250%	2.250%	2.250%
640 – 659	0.500%	1.250%	2.750%	3.000%	3.250%	2.750%	2.750%	2.750%
620 – 639	0.500%	1.500%	3.000%	3.000%	3.250%	3.250%	3.250%	3.500%
< 620(1)	0.500%	1.500%	3.000%	3.000%	3.250%	3.250%	3.250%	3.750%

Figure 125. FNMA LLPA matrix

Figure 125 is the LLPA matrix as provided by FNMA. We need to convert it to the rules-as-rows decision table of DMN Method and Style (Figure 126). Credit scores below 620 are ineligible for securitization, as are LTV values over 97%, so these entries are null in the decision table.

The output decision Rate just adds to the best rate one eighth of a percent per percent of LLPA, using a literal expression (Figure 127).

---

[26] https://www.fanniemae.com/content/pricing/llpa-matrix.pdf

A	p_Credit Score tCreditScore [300..850]	p_LTV tPercent	LLPA tPercent
1	>=740	<=60	0
2		[60..75]	0.25
3		[75..95]	0.5
4		[95..97]	0.75
5	[720..740)	<=60	0
6		[60..70]	0.25
7		[70..75]	0.5
8		[75..80]	0.75
9		[80..95]	0.5
10		[95..97]	1.0
11	[700..720)	<=60	0
12		[60..70]	0.5
13		[70..75]	1.0
14		[75..80]	1.25
15		[80..95]	1.0
16		[95..97]	1.5
17	[680..700)	<=60	0
18		[60..70]	0.5
19		[70..75]	1.25
20		[75..80]	1.75
21		[80..85]	1.5
22		[85..95]	1.25
23		[95..97]	1.5
24	[660..680)	<=60	0
25		[60..70]	1.0
26		[70..75]	2.25
27		[75..85]	2.75
28		[85..97]	2.25
29	[640..660)	<=60	0.5
30		[60..70]	1.25
31		[70..75]	2.75
32		[75..80]	3.0
33		[80..85]	3.25
34		[85..97]	2.75
35	[620..640)	<=60	0.5
36		[60..70]	1.5
37		[70..80]	3.0
38		[80..95]	3.25
39		[95..97]	3.5
40	<620	.	null
41	.	>97	null

Figure 126. *LLPA* decision table

Rate
tPercent

p_Best rate+0.125*LLPA

Figure 127. *Rate*

That completes the service definition implementing the *Loan rate* decision. Now we switch personas back to the modeler who didn't know how to model Loan rate. That person simply connects the service *Adjusted loan rate* to *Loan rate* with a knowledge requirement and defines the invocation (Figure 128). Since we have taken care to make the parameter names different from other model names, we avoid the situation of mapping a variable to itself. Note that the parameter prefixes *p_* are not import prefixes but are part of the parameter names, so they are retained in the boxed invocation.

Loan rate
tPercent

Adjusted loan rate

1	p_Best rate *tPercent*	Best rate
2	p_Credit Score *tCreditScore* *[300..850]*	Credit Score
3	p_LTV *tPercent*	LTV

Figure 128. *Loan rate* **invocation**

Modeling Multistep Decisions

Before finishing up on decision services, let's go back to the example that started it all, the multistep Lending decision from the DMN spec. We can use something like the decision service wizard to define the services and visualize each one on its own DRD page in the model. This reveals the multistep nature of the decision model, but to completely represent the end to end decision logic you still need a process model, sometimes called a *decision flow*, modeled as BPMN (Figure 129).

Decision Flows

Each activity in the decision flow represents a *decision point*, executing something in DMN. The icon in the upper left corner of the activity indicates its *task type*. The icon in the first two activities in Figure 129 identifies them as *decision tasks*, also called *business rule tasks*, meaning they invoke a *DMN decision service*. The head and shoulders icon denotes a *user task*, indicating a *human decision*. Although we don't have an example of it in the Lending decision, the decision flow could also include an activity with the gears icon denoting a *service task* invoking an *external decision*, some automated logic provided by an external system, not DMN.

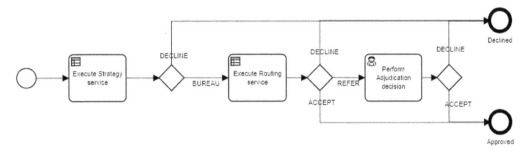

Figure 129. Decision flow for Lending decision

As discussed in Chapter 5, in the decision flow each task is followed by a *gateway*, the diamond shape, with one gate, or outgoing arrow, per possible value of the decision outcome. The gate label in the decision flow should match the output value in DMN.

The business decision as a whole is represented by the decision flow as a whole. The possible outcomes of the end to end decision are represented in the decision flow by the *end events*, the thick circles. Each end event label defines a *decision flow end state* and corresponds to an output value of the top-level decision in the DRD.

We can create decision flows like this using the Trisotech BPMN editor. Decision flows should contain only tasks that execute decisions, gateways with one gate per decision output value, and one end event for each outcome of the decision as a whole. Optionally you could add data objects in the process model, linked to each decision task, indicating the decision service parameters.

Spec Lending Example Revisited

The decision flow of Figure 129 reveals the steps of the Lending decision. First, we execute the *Strategy* decision service, which has outputs "BUREAU" and "DECLINE". If "BUREAU", we execute the *Routing* decision service; if "DECLINE", the top-level decision is "Declined". The *Routing* service has outputs "ACCEPT", "REFER", and "DECLINE". If "ACCEPT", the top-level decision is "Approved"; if "DECLINED", the top-level decision is "Declined"; if "REFER", we perform a human decision, resulting in either "Approved" or "Declined".

In Figure 130 once again we see the DRD from the DMN spec, with the boundaries of the *Strategy* and *Routing* services shown as thick bordered polygons. Information requirements crossing into those regions indicate the service parameters. Those polygons are just PowerPoint, not DMN, but overlaying rounded rectangles clearly would be difficult. Instead we use the decision service wizard define these services, identifying their output decisions, encapsulated decisions, and input parameters. These can be displayed in their own separate DRDs using the official rounded rectangle shape (Figure 131).

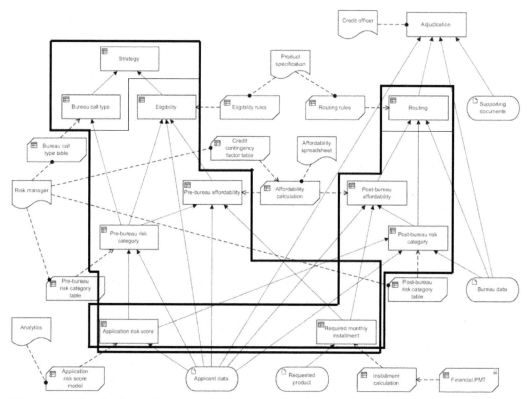

Figure 130. Service boundaries overlaid on Lending decision DRD

These diagrams of Figure 131 are from the DMN spec, but they would look similar in the Trisotech tool. The three dots in the decisions here mean that some information or knowledge requirements – such as invoked BKMs - are not shown in this diagram. In the Trisotech tool you can click on the three dots and insert the missing shapes in the DRD. The complete decision model would include the overall DRD plus these individual service DRDs. Remember, the same semantic element may be displayed in multiple diagrams. The individual service DRDs let you see clearly the inputs and enclosed elements of the two decision services, but to see how the decision as a whole fits together you also need a process diagram, the decision flow.

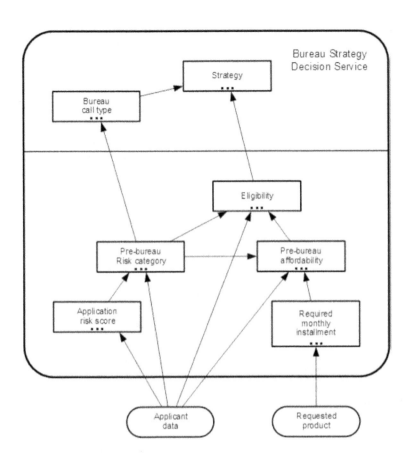

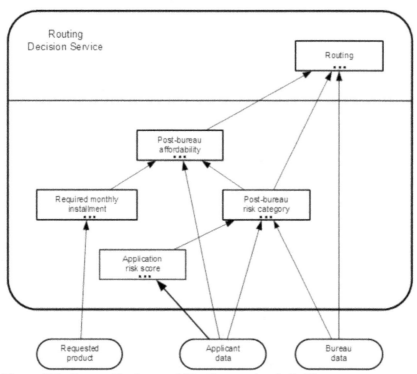

Figure 131. *Bureau Strategy* and *Routing* service definitions

CHAPTER 11

DMN Beyond the Basics

FEEL

The idea of executable decision models created by business is starting to freak out some traditional rule engine vendors. They will tell you that full DMN – notably its expression language FEEL - is really for programmers, not business. But that's not really true. Adoption by business users is a stated goal of DMN, and showing business users how to use the power of DMN is a fundamental goal of this book. Empowerment of business users to create complex decision models is possible because in DMN the decision logic is defined graphically, through diagrams and tables, not programming.

While FEEL can do quite a lot, it's just an expression language. FEEL just evaluates an expression to return a value. It does not create variables or assign and update their values. Those things in DMN are done graphically, by the implicit semantics of the DRD, decision tables and other boxed expressions. I need to emphasize this because it is often misrepresented as programming by vendors who don't want to implement it and practitioners who don't want to learn it.

I like to return to the example of Excel, which I mentioned in Chapter 2. In Excel, you point and click in a cell, and then type in a simple expression to calculate a value. Excel is clearly a tool for business users. But not all business users are the same. Almost all can create a table of numbers, add them up, make a chart of it. It's simple but actually the predominant use of the tool. Any business user can do that.

Then there's the Excel *Formulas menu* (Figure 132), containing what DMN would call *functions*. These functions calculate a value based on arguments you enter, and expressions containing the function assign that value to the cell. The arguments – that is, the inputs to the formula – are typically not variable names but other cells, identified by their grid position, like A1 or C23. Formulas are a key tool of power users in the business, but they are not programming. They are just an expression language that calculates values, just like FEEL.

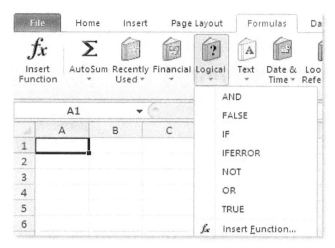

Figure 132. Formulas ribbon in Excel

Excel *macros* (Figure 133) are something else. That's programming. They are more powerful than Formulas, but they're not for business users. DMN in all its glory – FEEL, BKMs, and all the boxed expressions – is like Excel Formulas not macros. It is not programming.

```
(General)                                                    ▼   Macro1

    Sub Macro1()
    '
    ' Macro1 Macro
    '


    '
        Windows("Stocks_Ground.xlsm").Activate
        Windows("Stocks_Ground.xlsm").Activate
        Windows("Stocks_Ground.xlsm").Activate
    End Sub

    Function StockQuote(strTicker As String, Optional dtDate As Variant)
    ' Date is optional - if omitted, use today. If value is not a date, throw
    If IsMissing(dtDate) Then
    dtDate = Date
    Else
    If Not (IsDate(dtDate)) Then
    StockQuote = CVErr(xlErrNum)
    End If
    End If

    Dim dtPrevDate As Date
```

Figure 133. Excel macro

That means decision models in DMN are not merely business requirements handed off to programmers in some other language. DMN itself is an executable language. You can execute the model right in the modeling tool to see if the logic makes sense. And you can deploy it to a cloud service, where you provide the input values and the service returns the result!

While DMN decision logic is defined in diagrams and tables, to make it executable and tool-independent, the text in those diagrams and tables requires a *standard expression language* with precisely defined grammar. Now we're getting to the heart of the matter, because that language needs to be both business-friendly and at the same time rich enough to handle real-world decision logic, not just the simple tests performed in decision tables.

The original DMN task force struggled with this. Some were against specifying any formal expression language. Some wanted their own rule language. In the end, the task force came up with FEEL, which stands for *Friendly Enough Expression Language*, a brand new expression language, along with standardized tabular formats called *boxed expressions* for assembling those expressions into something like program statements. In combination, boxed expressions and FEEL create a powerful decision language, in which the logic is described entirely in diagrams and tables yet is executable on a DMN engine.

As an expression language, FEEL simply defines formulas for computing a value. It is not a full programming language. It does not create variables, assign values to them, or maintain the running state of the model in execution. Those things are performed by the DRD and boxed expressions. FEEL expressions can reference variables, but in they end they just calculate a value.

Like other languages, FEEL is defined as a set of formal grammar rules (Figure 134). Such a grammar allows tools to parse and compile FEEL expressions into executable form. Red Hat Drools, a leading decision engine, has made their FEEL runtime open source, and it has already been incorporated into several DMN tools, including Trisotech DMN Modeler.

10.3.1.2   Grammar rules

The complete FEEL grammar is specified below. Grammar rules are numbered, and in some cases alternatives are lettered, for later reference. Boxed expression syntax (rule 55) is used to give execution semantics to boxed expressions.

1. expression =
    a. textual expression |
    b. boxed expression ;

2. textual expression =
    a. function definition | for expression | if expression | quantified expression |
    b. disjunction |
    c. conjunction |
    d. comparison |
    e. arithmetic expression |
    f. instance of |
    g. path expression |
    h. filter expression | function invocation |
    i. literal | simple positive unary test | name | "(" , textual expression , ")" ;

3. textual expressions = textual expression , { "," , textual expression } ;

4. arithmetic expression =
    a. addition | subtraction |
    b. multiplication | division |
    c. exponentiation |
    d. arithmetic negation ;

5. simple expression = arithmetic expression | simple value ;

6. simple expressions = simple expression , { "," , simple expression } ;

7. simple positive unary test =
    a. ["<" | "<=" | ">" | ">="] , endpoint |
    b. interval ;

8. interval = (open interval start | closed interval start) , endpoint , ".." , endpoint , (open interval end | closed interval end) ;

9. open interval start = "(" | ")" ;

10. closed interval start = "[" ;

11. open interval end = ")" | "[" ;

12. closed interval end = "]" ;

13. simple positive unary tests = simple positive unary test , { "," , simple positive unary test } ;

14. simple unary tests =
    a. simple positive unary tests |
    b. "not", "(", simple positive unary tests, ")" |

Figure 134. FEEL grammar in DMN spec

Boxed Expressions

Recapping from earlier in the book, each decision in the DRD is represented by a *variable*, and the decision's *value expression* calculates its value. DMN defines several types of value expressions, each with its own boxed expression format. So far, we've discussed three of them:

- Decision table

- Literal expression

- Invocation

There are also three more:

- Function definition, usually implemented as a BKM, representing parameterized decision logic

- Context, which breaks down a complex value expression into a list of simpler ones, called context entries

- Relation, a table of expressions, usually used to embed static data tables inside a decision model.

The logic of each of these value expression types is defined graphically as a boxed expression. These defined tabular formats are an integral part of the DMN language, so a tool that doesn't support them really doesn't implement DMN. Most are basically 2-column tables. The first column, shaded, names a variable; the second column is its value expression, usually a FEEL literal expression but possibly a nested boxed expression, such as invocation or even a decision table. In this part of the book we'll learn how to use all of them.

CHAPTER 12

Literal Expressions

Values vs Expressions

In DMN, a literal expression means some text in the FEEL language that when evaluated returns a value. Unless you are entering input data values in the Test Run dialog, when you type something into a decision table or literal expression, you are entering a FEEL *expression*, not a value. A FEEL expression enclosed in quotes, for example "High", evaluates to the literal text value enclosed by the quotes, or High. The text value itself does not include the quotation marks, so, for example, you would not include them in when entering an input value in the Test Run dialog. On the other hand, the FEEL expression High, not enclosed in quotes, does not mean the literal text value High. Without quotes, High is a *name* – the name of a variable, typically representing a decision or input data element, so the value of High, without quotes, is the value of that decision or input data. A name may not begin with a digit.

FEEL	Value	Type
"High"	High	Text
High	Value of the variable named High	Type of the variable named High
0	0	Number
"0"	0	Text
1974-09-03	1962	Number
"1974-09-03"	1974-09-03	Text
date("1974-09-03")	1974-09-03	Date
true	true	Boolean
"true"	true	Text

Figure 135. Values vs FEEL expressions

A FEEL expression for a literal numeric value is just that number; the value and the FEEL expression are the same. The FEEL expression "0" in quotes does not mean the number zero. It means the text string 0.

A date value requires the format YYYY-MM-DD, defined by an ISO standard, such as 1974-09-03. In the Test Run dialog, you would enter that format for the input data element *Date of Birth*. But in FEEL, you would enter something different: date("1974-09-03"),which is the *date* constructor function applied to a literal string value in the ISO date format. If you omit the constructor function but include the quotes, it means the text string 1974-09-03. And if you omit the quotes, FEEL interprets that as subtraction, giving the number 1962, possibly not what you meant. Similar rules apply to times and durations.

The FEEL expression true without quotes is not a variable name; it is a reserved word for a Boolean value. If you put quotes around it, it means the literal text value true – a string type, not a Boolean

Literal Expression Elements

While DMN allows an implementation to use expression languages other than FEEL, doing that breaks the promise of a tool-independent standard. So when I say literal expression, I always mean a FEEL literal expression. The expression references constants, variables, and functions.

Constants, or *literal values*, include several types: text strings enclosed in quotes; numbers; Boolean values, true or false; and date/time literals to represent dates, times, and durations. The latter require a constructor function, like *date()*, with an appropriately formatted text string within the parentheses; And there is a special constant, *null*, meaning nothing – no value, or possibly an error.

Variables represent *named values*, typically the value of a decision, BKM, or input data element. You reference variables by their *name*. DMN variables include structured data, a business object containing components, and you reference components of those variables by their *qualified name* using a dot notation. For example, *Applicant.lastName* means the component *lastName* of the structured variable – let's say input data element – *Applicant*.

Functions are named expressions based on variables called *parameters*. Functions allow reuse of decision logic. Each *invocation* of the function supplies values to the parameters, and the function returns an output value. Previously we've encountered function invocation as a boxed expression mapping decision inputs to the parameters of a BKM or decision service, but we can also embed function invocation directly inside a literal expression. The syntax of such a *literal invocation* is the function *name* followed by a list of parameter value expressions, called *arguments*, enclosed in parentheses. For example, suppose the BKM *Loan Amortization Formula*, which we've seen previously, has parameters *p*, the loan amount; *r*, the loan rate, and *n*, the loan term, defined in that order. In that case the literal expression for *Loan payment* might be written as

```
Loan Amortization Formula(myLoan.amount, myLoan.ratePct/100, 360)
```

In this syntax, values are passed to parameters in their defined *order*, not by name. So if *myLoan* is an input to *Loan payment*, the value *myLoan.amount* is mapped to the first parameter *p*, *myLoan.ratePct*/100 is mapped to the second parameter *r*, and the literal value 360 is mapped to the third parameter, *n*.

Anything in a FEEL expression that is not a constant, a variable, or a function is an *operator*. FEEL operators include special reserved words such as *if, then, else, and, or*, etc., and symbols like +, -, *, [, etc. When FEEL is executed, the software must parse the text and determine what is a variable, what is a function, what is an operator. This is not so easy because valid names in FEEL may contain spaces, and under certain conditions also operator characters. This allows decision names to be more user-friendly, but it makes implementation of FEEL more difficult for tool vendors.

One thing that simplifies parsing of FEEL is the fact that a value expression may only reference *names in scope*. For a decision, those are limited to its *information requirements* and *knowledge requirements*, and typically there are just a few of those. For a BKM or decision service, names in scope include only *parameters* plus any invocations of other BKMs or services, modeled as *knowledge requirements*.

Functions

In a literal expression, a name followed by parentheses enclosing a list of literal expressions represents a *function*.

DMN has two types of functions: *Built-in functions* are part of the FEEL language. Their parameters and behavior are defined in the DMN spec, not in the decision model. For example, the functions *sum*, summing a list of numbers, or *not*, negating a Boolean expression, are built-in functions. Built-in function names are reserved words in FEEL; a variable name may not start with the name of a built-in function. BKMs and decision services represent *modeler-defined functions*. Unlike built-in functions, their names, parameters, and logic are defined in the model. The *name* of the function is the name of the BKM or decision service, which is also the name of its associated variable.

Parameters

For both types of functions, *parameters* are variables named by the function as part of the *function definition*. Each parameter has a name and a datatype. Recall that a boxed invocation maps values to parameters *by name*, whereas literal invocation maps values to parameters *by their order in the function definition*. It is highly unusual to use boxed invocation with a built-in function, although it is technically allowed. Almost always, built-in functions use literal invocation, so the *names* of built-in function parameters are rarely used. With built-in functions, what is more important than the parameter name is the *count* of parameters, their *order*, and their *datatype*.

For example, the Boolean function *not()* has a single parameter, *negand*, which is a Boolean type, and the action of *not* is to change false to true and true to false. Some built-in functions have variants based on the count of parameters. For example, one form of the list function *sum* has a single parameter, *list*, a variable whose type is a list of numbers. Another form of *sum* has multiple parameters, *b1*, *b2*, and so forth, each of which must be a number. They both do the same thing, which is to sum the numbers in the list.

For some functions, the behavior depends on the count of parameters. For example, *substring* with two parameters extracts the portion of the first parameter, *string*, beginning at the character *start position*, the second parameter. But *substring* with a third parameter, *length*, only extracts the count of characters specified by *length*.

Arguments

With literal invocation of a function, the comma-separated list of expressions inside parentheses are called *arguments*. Each argument is a value expression for a function parameter. Here are some examples:

Suppose we have input data *myList*, a list of numbers: 1,2,3. Here the expression *sum(myList)* says that we are passing the list of numbers 1,2,and 3 to the function, which is going to add them together, giving 6. In this function, *myList* is the argument of the function *sum*, i.e. the value of its single parameter, *list*.

An argument is not necessarily just a name or literal value. It could be an expression. For example, *not* has a single parameter, a Boolean. So the expression *not(Risk="High")* takes the Boolean expression *Risk="High"*, which could be true or false, and negates it. It's true if the variable *Risk* does not have the value High.

Note with literal invocation, the parameter *names*, *list* and *negand*, are not used at all. With literal invocation, we just reference the *arguments*, the value expressions for each parameter inside the parentheses. The parameter names don't matter, but what does matter is their *order*. The first argument means the value of the first parameter, and so on. The order of the arguments MUST BE the same as the order of parameters in the function definition.

The functions *sum* and *not* both have a single parameter, but a built-in function like *list contains* has two parameters: *list*, the name of a variable representing a list; and *value*, an item value. With literal invocation we don't care about the parameter names, *list* and *value*. We just care that there are two parameters, the first one being a list, the second one being an item value possibly contained in the list. *list contains* is a Boolean function. It's true if the list variable named by the first argument contains the value specified by the second argument. So to test whether the variable *myList* contains the value *0*, we would write

```
list contains(myList, 0),
```

using the argument values not the parameter names.

My friend Edson Tirelli, who created Red Hat's DMN runtime, asks that I mention that technically it is possible with literal invocation to pass argument values by parameter name, using the syntax quoted parameter name, colon, value, for each parameter, like this:

```
list contains("value": 0, "list": myList)
```

and that it is not necessary to respect the defined parameter order when doing it this way. Although this FEEL syntax is of more interest to computer scientists like Edson than normal decision modelers, it will execute properly on a DMN engine.

We've seen how the Trisotech expression editor tries to help you with the expression syntax, names in scope, etc. But if you use a function, the editor still expects you to know the order and datatype of the arguments, and the datatype of the function output. It won't warn you about those errors.

Operators

Operators in a literal expression include symbols and other special names *not* followed by a parenthesized list of arguments. The syntax of expressions including operators is strictly defined by the FEEL grammar.

The meaning of some operators, like + and >, depends on the datatype of the *operands*, the expressions preceding and/or following the operator. The + operator, for example, means addition if the operands are numbers but concatenation if they are strings. The expression 1+1 returns the number value 2, but the expression "1" + "1" returns the string value 11. Similarly, the operator > is type-dependent. If *a* and *b* are numbers, the expression *a>b* is true if *a* is greater than *b*, but if they are strings it tests alphabetical order.

Operators also include reserved words like *if* and *for* with special meaning. The *if* operator is used in *if..then..else* literal expressions, conditional logic. For example (Figure 136), suppose *Loan Approval* is "Approved" if *Risk Category* is "Medium" or "Low" and *is Affordable* is true, otherwise "Declined".

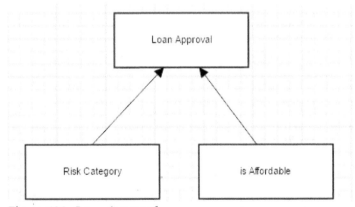

Figure 136. *Loan Approval*

We could model it as a decision table, of course, but we can also model it as a literal expression using *if..then..else*:

```
if (Risk Category="Medium" or Risk Category="Low") and is
Affordable = true then "Approved" else "Declined"
```

Alternatively, incorporating the in and { ,] operators, we can write it as:

```
if Risk Category in ["Medium", "Low"] and is Affordable = true
then "Approved" else "Declined"
```

The *for* operator is used in iteration with the syntax *for..in..return*. We'll discuss iteration and other aspects of lists and tables in Chapter 15.

FEEL String Functions

The FEEL built-in functions operating on strings is shown in Figure 137. Some return a string, some return a Boolean value, others a number or a list of strings.

Function name	Result type	1st parameter (type)	2nd parameter (type)	3rd parameter (type)	
substring	String	string (string)	start position (number)	length? (number)	substring("abc",1,2)="ab"
string length	Number	string (string)			string length("abc")=3
upper case, lower case	String	string (string)			upper case("abc")="ABC"
substring before, substring after	String	string (string)	match (string		substring before("abc","c")="ab"
contains	Boolean	string (string)	match (string)		contains("abc", "x")=false
starts with, ends with	Boolean	string (string)	match (string)		starts with("abc", "a")=true
matches	Boolean	string (string)	pattern (string – Regex)	flags? (string)	matches("abc", "[a-z]{3}")=true
replace	String	string (string)	pattern (string – Regex)	replacement, flags? (string)	replace("abc", "b", "*")="a*c"
split	String list	string (string)	Delimiter (string – Regex)		Split("John Doe", "\\s") = ["John", "Doe"]
number	Number	from (string)	grouping separator (string): space, comma, period, or null	decimal separator (string): period, comma, or null	number("12,345.67", ",", ".") = 12345.67

Figure 137. FEEL built-in string functions

Remember, the names of the parameters are unimportant. Their count, order, and datatypes are what counts. Optional parameters are indicated by a question mark. The last column provides an example of the function.

- *substring* extracts a new string starting at the position of argument 2, and if a third argument is provided, containing that number of characters.

- *string length* returns the number of characters in the string.

- *upper case* and *lower case* convert all characters to upper or lower case.

- *substring before* and *substring after* extract the string occurring either before or after the match string.

- *contains* is a Boolean test, returning true if the first argument contains the second argument.

- *starts with* and *ends with* are also Boolean tests, whether the input string starts with or ends with the match string.

- *matches* and *replace* are powerful string analysis and manipulation functions using so-called *regular expressions*. Regular expressions allow you to find and replace *character patterns* in the string. The examples on this slide are very simple, but the full scope of regular expressions is too complicated to explain here. A good reference is rexegg.com.

- *split* converts a delimited text string into a list of strings. The delimiter is defined as a regular expression.

- *number* converts a string representation of a number to a FEEL number and supports international variants of that representation. The *grouping separator*, either a space, comma, period, or null, meaning none, is the separator between thousands in a large number; for example, in USA, this is normally a comma. In the USA, the *decimal separator*, either period or comma, is normally a period.

FEEL Number Functions

FEEL built-in functions taking a single number as argument are listed in Figure 138.

- *floor* and *ceiling* return the greatest integer lower than or equal to the number, or smallest integer greater than or equal to the number.

- *decimal* rounds the number to the number of decimal places indicated by the second argument.

- *abs* returns the absolute value of the number.

- *modulo* returns the remainder after dividing the first argument by the second.

- *sqrt* returns the square root of the number.

- *log* returns the natural logarithm of the number.

- *exp* returns Euler's constant e (2.718…) raised to the number power.

- *odd* and *even* return a Boolean test of whether the number is odd or even, respectively.

- *string* converts the number to a string.

Function name	Result type	1st parameter	2nd parameter	3rd parameter	
floor	number	number			floor(1.5)=1
ceiling	number	number			ceiling(1.5)=2
decimal	number	number	scale (number)		decimal(1.5763,2) = 1.58 decimal(3/2, 2) = 1.50 = 1.5
abs	number	number			abs(-10) = 10
string	string	from (number)			string(2) + string(2) = 22 (a string)
modulo	number	dividend (number)	divisor (number)		modulo(12, 5) = 2
sqrt	number	number			sqrt(4) = 2
log	number	number			log(10) = 2.30258509299
exp	number	number			exp(5) = 148.413159102577
odd	Boolean	number			odd(5) = true
even	Boolean	number			even(5) = false

Figure 138. FEEL built-in number functions

Note that the exponentiation operator ** only works with integers, i.e. $a**b$ (a to the bth power) is defined only for integer values of b. But the functions exp and log, added in DMN 1.2, allow a workaround, $exp(b*log(a))$, which is valid for non-integer b.

Formatting Numbers

FEEL provides a function to convert a formatted number to a string, but not the other way around. You may have noticed that numeric formulas in FEEL return an unformatted number, usually with too many digits after the decimal point, and you'd rather see a more presentable format. Let's say you want to format *Loan payment* with a currency symbol, thousands separator, and two digits after the decimal point. It is possible to do this entirely in FEEL, but very complicated and not worth the effort. A much better way is to invoke the Java *format* method as a BKM.

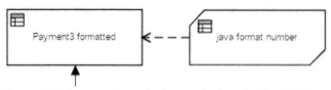

Figure 139. Java static methods may be invoked as BKMs

In Figure 139, *Payment3 formatted* takes an unformatted number and invokes the BKM *java format number* (Figure 140). The J in the upper left means this BKM is a Java static method.

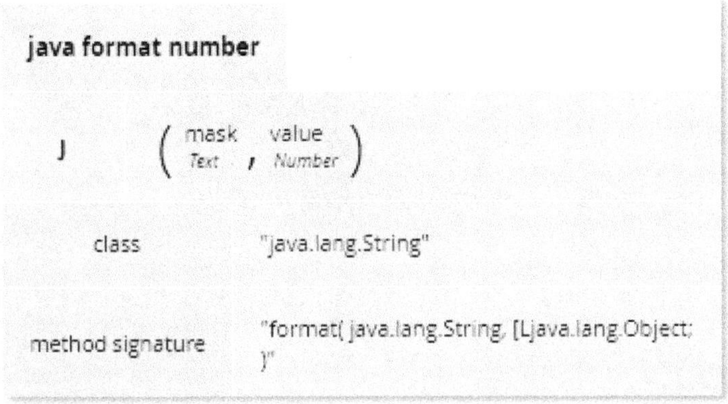

Figure 140. *java format number* **converts number to a formatted string**

The DMN spec specifies the boxed invocation of a Java static method as shown in Figure 140, defining the Java *class* and *method signature*. The *class* we want to format a number to a string is "java.lang.String", and the *method signature* is

"format(java.lang.String, [Ljava.lang.Object;)"

This method takes a numeric *value* and a *mask*, a text string encoding how we want it formatted. The *mask* and the *value* are passed to this BKM by invocation (Figure 141). The value is the input to *Payment3 formatted*, called *Monthly Payment3*. The mask is the string "$%,4.2f", which means start with the currency symbol $, use comma as the thousands separator, and round to 2 digits after the decimal point.

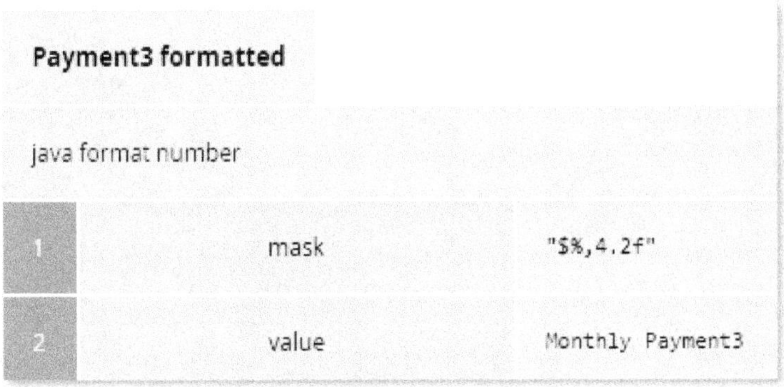

Figure 141. Boxed invocation of *java format number*

We use this mask a lot in formatting currency amounts! As we showed in the first part of the book, business users don't have to know how to derive these complicated formulas, just how to invoke them.

CHAPTER 13

Contexts

Perhaps the most misunderstood boxed expression type is called a *context*. Contexts are actually quite useful in simplifying the process logic and extending the scope of logic reuse. In this chapter we'll see how to use them.

In Figure 142, *Monthly Payment* invokes the BKM *payment* – our old friend the Loan Amortization Formula – using the inputs *Loan*, a structure including components *rate, term, pointsPct*, and *fees*; *Purchase price*; and *downAmt*. We use *Purchase price, downAmt, pointsPct*, and *fees* to calculate the loan amount.

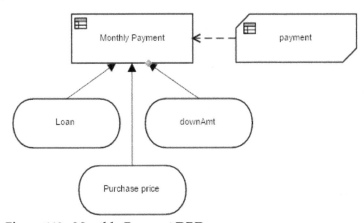

Figure 142. *Monthly Payment* **DRD**

We could do this in a single literal invocation, embedding the loan amount calculation in the expression for the first argument (Figure 143). The DRD is small, but the literal expression is complicated, maybe too hard to understand.

Monthly Payment

```
payment((Purchase price-downAmt)*(1+Loan.pointsPct/100)+Loan.fees,Loan.rate,Loan.term)
```

Figure 143. *Monthly Payment* **as a complex literal expression**

We can simplify the invocation expression by inserting the supporting decision *Loan Amount* in the DRD (Figure 144).

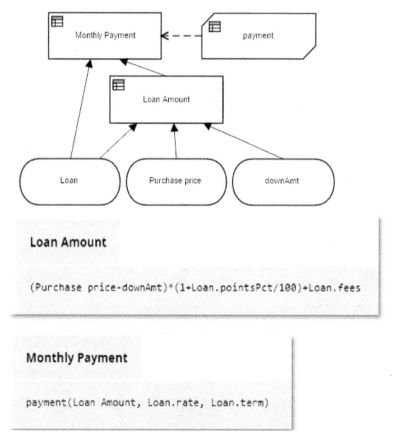

Loan Amount

```
(Purchase price-downAmt)*(1+Loan.pointsPct/100)+Loan.fees
```

Monthly Payment

```
payment(Loan Amount, Loan.rate, Loan.term)
```

Figure 144. Adding supporting decision simplifies the expressions but adds DRD element

Most business users would say this is better. And in a real decision model, we always have this tradeoff: We can simplify the literal expressions by inserting more supporting decisions in the DRD. But this only works up to a point, since too many of these supporting decisions eventually clutter up the DRD to the point where the overall decision logic becomes hard to manage. Contexts are an answer to this problem. They provide a way to simplify literal expressions without excessively proliferating DRD elements.

Simplifying the Decision Logic

A context is a value expression type, with its own tabular boxed expression format, in which the table rows, called *context entries*, act like supporting decisions. Each context entry defines a variable local to that decision – so you don't worry if it has the same name as a variable outside the decision – that you can use in the decision's value expression, simplifying its logic. Here is an example.

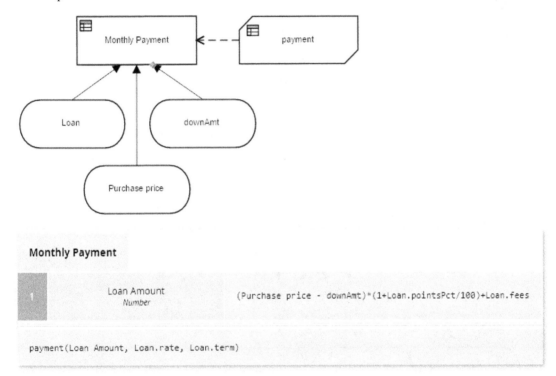

Figure 145. *Monthly Payment* **as a context**

Our DRD is once again simple and the literal expressions in the boxed context (Figure 145) are simple as well. In a boxed context, the first column is the context entry name and type. Here we only have one, *Loan Amount*, a number. The right column is an expression for that variable. Here it is a literal expression, but it could be a decision table, invocation, or a nested context. The last row, called the *final result box*, has no context entry name, just an expression that returns the value of the context.

We previously discussed the names in scope of a value expression, which are normally the information requirements (or, for a BKM, the parameters) plus any knowledge requirements. But for a context, we have additional names in scope, which are the names of the *prior context entries* of this context. And this is what simplifies the decision logic, because we can define the context entry *Loan Amount* as a formula and then reference the variable *Loan Amount* in the final result.

This is a nice compromise. This example just has just one context entry plus the final result box, but in general a context may have many more. Contexts allow modelers to use fewer decision nodes in the DRD without requiring long and complex literal expressions.

Consider the following example. We want the decision logic to calculate the *Total Price* of an order item, to include applicable discounts, tax, and shipping cost. The input data are *Quantity*, *Unit Price, isTaxable* (a Boolean), and *Shipping Type*, either "Standard" or "Rush". The rules are as follows:

- *Price before discount = Quantity * Unit Price*

- *Price after discount =* if *Quantity* >6 then 0.90**Price before discount* else *Price before discount*

- *Tax =* if *isTaxable* is **true** then 0.09**Price after discount* else 0

- *Shipping*

  o   If *Shipping Type* = "Standard" and *Price after discount* <100 then 9.95

  o   If *Shipping Type* = "Standard" and *Price after discount* >=100 then 0

  o   If *Shipping Type* = "Rush" then 17.95

Using a context, we can model this logic in a single decision (Figure 146):

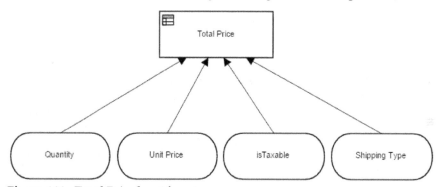

Figure 146. *Total Price* **has 4 inputs**

The boxed context (Figure 147) calculates *Price before discount, Price after discount, Tax,* and *Shipping cost* as separate context entries, and the final result box computes the total cost. Note that the expression for the *Shipping cost* context entry is a decision table, and that one of the inputs to *Shipping cost* is the previous context entry *Price after discount*.

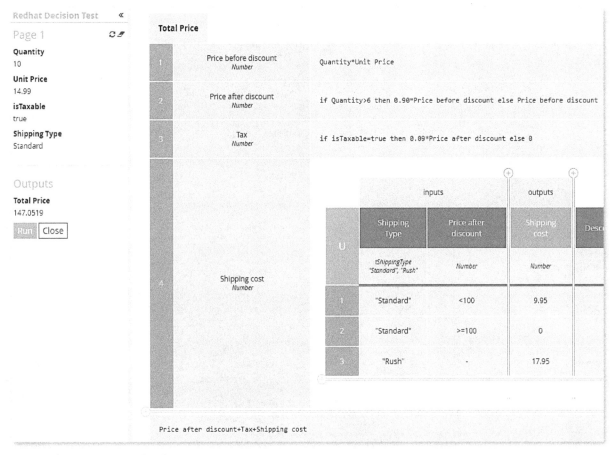

Total Price

1	Price before discount *Number*	Quantity*Unit Price	
2	Price after discount *Number*	if Quantity>6 then 0.90*Price before discount else Price before discount	
3	Tax *Number*	if isTaxable=true then 0.09*Price after discount else 0	

Redhat Decision Test «

Page 1

Quantity
10

Unit Price
14.99

isTaxable
true

Shipping Type
Standard

Outputs

Total Price
147.0519

Run | Close

		inputs		outputs	
U		Shipping Type	Price after discount	Shipping cost	Desc
		tShippingType "Standard", "Rush"	*Number*	*Number*	
	1	"Standard"	<100	9.95	
	2	"Standard"	>=100	0	
	3	"Rush"	-	17.95	

4 | Shipping cost
Number

Price after discount+Tax+Shipping cost

Figure 147. *Total Price* **as a context**

Creating Structured Variables

A context is not required to have a final result box. In a context without a final result box, the final result is a data structure with one component per context entry. Thus, a context is the usual way to model a decision in which the output is a structured variable. Building on the previous example, suppose we want to return not just the total price but its components, for example, as columns in an invoice, using the structure *tInvoice* (Figure 148).

The solution couldn't be simpler. Just make *Total Price* a normal context entry and omit the final result box (Figure 149). Now other decisions can separately reference *Invoice.Total Price*, *Invoice.Shipping cost*, or any other component.

	1	Price before discount	Number
	2	Price after discount	Number
tInvoice	3	Tax	Number
	4	Shipping cost	Number
	5	Total Price	Number

Figure 148. Structure of *tInvoice*

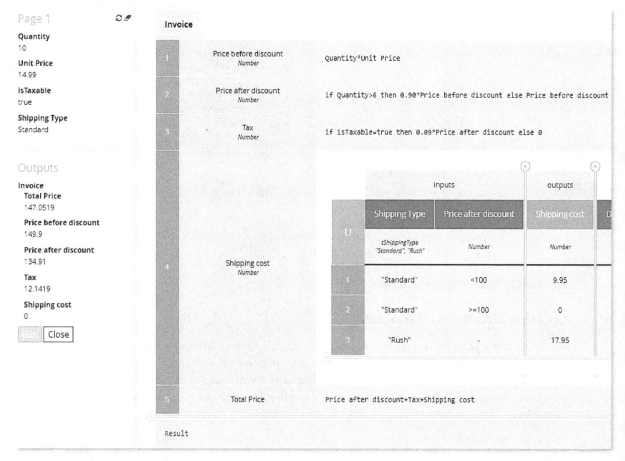

Figure 149. *Invoice* as context with no final result box

BKMs with Context

We previously discussed an important difference between a BKM and a decision service is that while the service may be modeled as a DRD, a BKM is always a single value expression. In practice, this difference is modest because we can always model the BKM as a context. In such a BKM, the context entries can reference the BKM parameters – shown in parentheses above the context entries – plus prior context entries, plus any BKMs that the BKM itself invokes.

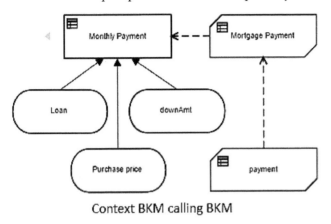

Context BKM calling BKM

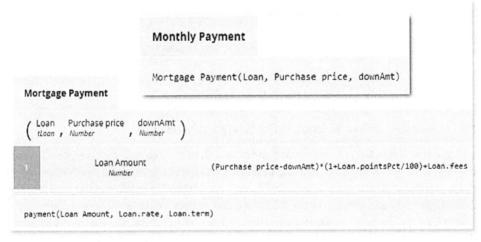

Figure 150. BKM as a context

In Figure 150, for example, the decision *Monthly Payment* invokes the BKM *Mortgage Payment*, a context that calculates the *Loan Amount* and then calls another BKM, *payment*. DMN gives you many ways to model the same decision logic, building on reusable fragments as needed.

Context Entry as a Function Definition

We've seen that BKMs and decision services are examples of *function definitions*. These are modeled as elements of a Decision Requirements Diagram, but you can also define a context entry as a function definition, with its own boxed expression format.

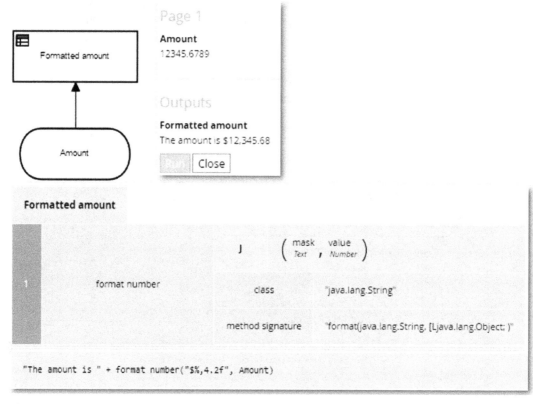

Figure 151. *format number* **as a function definition in a context entry**

This lets you define a function in one context entry and then invoke it in a subsequent context entry or in the final result box. A common use of this is with Java static methods such as formatting a number as a string, discussed in Chapter 12. Instead of modeling the Java method as a BKM, which adds an element to the DRD, we can simply make it a context entry, as in Figure 151. Here the decision *Formatted amount* is a context in which the first context entry, *format number*, is a function definition, and the final result box invokes that function in a literal expression. This type of construct is of interest primarily to more technical modelers, and other advanced examples of this kind may be found in the *DMN Cookbook*.

CHAPTER 14

Calendar Arithmetic

The ability to understand and manipulate dates and times, what I call calendar arithmetic, is very useful in a decision language, and FEEL supports that. The formats for dates, times, and durations look strange, but don't blame FEEL. They are a subset of the formats defined by the international standard *ISO 8601*, used for dates and times in many computer languages. Date, time, and duration literal values entered in the run dialog or reported as execution outputs use the ISO representation directly. FEEL expressions for dates, times, and durations require a constructor function with ISO format enclosed in quotes as its argument.

Date and time format - ISO 8601

What can ISO 8601 do for me?

ISO 8601 can be used by anyone who wants to use a standardized way of presenting dates and times. It helps cut out the uncertainty and confusion when communicating internationally.

The full standard covers ways to write:

- Date
- Time of day
- Coordinated universal time (UTC)
- Local time with offset to UTC
- Date and time
- Time intervals
- Recurring time intervals

How can I get ISO 8601?

You can buy the full standard from the ISO Store, or from the ISO member in your country.

What is ISO 8601?

ISO 8601 describes an internationally accepted way to represent dates and times using numbers.

When dates are represented with numbers they can be interpreted in different ways. For

Figure 152. ISO 8601 defines date, time, and duration syntax

Figure 153 illustrates the ISO formats for dates and times. A date is a 4-digit year, hyphen, 2-digit month, hyphen, 2-digit day. For example, May 3, 2017, as an input data value, is entered as 2015-05-03. But in a FEEL expression, you must write date("2017-05-03").

	ISO Format	String Value	FEEL Expression
Date	YYYY-MM-DD	2017-05-03	date("2017-05-03")
Time (local time)	hh:mm:ss	13:10:30	time("13:10:30")
Time (with timezone)	hh:mm:ss<offset>	13:10:30-07:00	time("13:10:30-07:00")
Time (UTC)	hh:mm:ssZ	20:10:30Z	time("20:10:30Z")
Date-Time (local time)	YYYY-MM-DDThh:mm:ss	2017-05-03T13:10:30	date and time("2017-05-03T13:10:30")
Date-Time (with timezone)	YYYY-MM-DDThh:mm:ss<offset>	2017-05-03T13:10:30-07:00	date and time("2017-05-03T13:10:30-07:00")
Date-Time (UTC)	YYYY-MM-DDThh:mm:ssZ	2017-05-03T20:10:30Z	date and time("2017-05-03T20:10:30Z")

Figure 153. ISO 8601 formats and corresponding FEEL expressions

Time is based on a 24-hour clock, no am/pm. The format is a 2-digit hour, colon, 2-digit minute, colon, 2-digit second, with optional fractional seconds after the decimal point. There is also an optional *time offset* field, the timezone expressed as an offset from UTC, formerly called Greenwich Mean Time. For example, in Los Angeles I am on Pacific Daylight Time, which is UTC – 7 hours, so to include my timezone I would write 13:10:30-07:00 as an input data value, or time("13:10:30-07:00") in a FEEL expression. To specify the time as UTC, I can either use 00:00:00 as the time offset, or the letter Z, which stands for Zulu, which is the military standard.

Date-time values concatenate the date and time formats with a capital T separating them. In a FEEL expression, you must use the proper constructor function with the ISO text string enclosed in quotes. The spec says that in a boxed expression, such as a decision table, a tool may omit the constructor function and quotes if the ISO string is shown in bold italics. Trisotech right now doesn't do that.

Date and Time Components

It is possible in FEEL to extract the year, month, or day component from a date or date-time using a dot notation. For example,

```
date("2017-05-03").year
```

returns the number 2017. Similarly, you can extract the hour, minute, or second component from a time or date-time using the dot notation. For example,

```
time("12:00:00-07:00").second
```

returns the number 0,

```
date and time("2016-12-09T15:37:00-08:00").hour
```

returns the number 15, and

```
date and time("2016-12-09T15:37:00-08:00").time offset
```

returns *duration("-PT8H")*. The interesting one is time offset, since extracting this component gives not a number but a duration, with a strange format we'll discuss shortly. The time offset duration must be between -14 hours and +14 hours. Alternatively, the *timezone* component

```
date and time("2016-12-09T15:37:00-08:00").timezone
```

returns the string "America/Los_Angeles", the IANA timezone identifier.

The *weekday* component was added in DMN 1.2, extracting an integer representing the day of the week, where 1 is Monday and 7 is Sunday.

Type Conversion

The *date* constructor function converts an ISO date string to a date. It also converts a date-time value to a date, omitting the time value. And if it has three number arguments, representing year, month, and day, the *date* function converts those to a date.

The *time* constructor function converts an ISO time string to a time. It also converts a date-time value to a time, omitting the date value. And if it has four arguments, numbers for hours, minutes, and seconds, and a duration for timezone, it converts that to a time.

The *date and time* constructor function converts an ISO date-time or date string to a date-time. And if it has two arguments, a date and a time – not strings but a FEEL date and a time – it converts those to a date-time.

Durations

The interval between two dates, times, or date-times defines a *duration*. DMN, like ISO, defines two kinds of duration, *days and time duration* and *years and months duration*.

Days and time duration is equivalent to the number of seconds in the duration. The ISO format is

```
PdDThHmMsS
```

where the lower case d,h,m, and s are replaced by integers indicating the days, hours, minutes, and seconds in the duration. If any of them is zero, they are omitted along with the corresponding uppercase D, H, M, or S. They are supposed to be normalized so that the sum of the component values is minimized. For example, a duration of 61 seconds should be written PT1M1S. That is the ISO string value. In a FEEL expression, you need to enclose that in quotes and make it the argument of the *duration* constructor function, *duration("PT1M1S")*.

For long durations, we use years and months duration, equivalent to the number of whole months included in the duration. The ISO format is

```
PyYmM
```

where lower case y and m are again replaced by integers representing number of years and months in the duration. Again, the normalized form minimizes the sum of those component values, so a duration of 14 months would be written in FEEL as *duration("P1Y2M")*. The calculation of years and months duration is the number of months in between the start date and the end date, plus 1 if the day of the end month is greater than or equal to the day of the start month, or plus zero otherwise.

As with dates and times, you can extract the components of a duration using a dot notation. For days and time duration, the components are days, hours, minutes, and seconds. For example,

```
duration("P1DT2H3M4S").days
```

returns the number 1.

For years and months duration, the components are years and months. For example,

```
duration("P1Y2M").months
```

returns the number 2.

The constructor function *duration* converts an ISO duration string either to a years and months duration or a days and time duration. The *years and months duration* constructor function does not take a string argument but instead two date-times, a start and an end, and it generates a years and months duration for that interval.

Date-Time Arithmetic

All this is background for the calendar arithmetic used in decision logic. Only certain combinations of dates, times, datetimes, durations, and numbers are allowed.

Addition

You can add a days and time duration to a date-time, date, or time, returning another date-time, date, or time, respectively. You can also add a years and months duration to a date-time or date, returning another date-time or date, respectively. And you can add two durations of the same type – days and time or years and months – to get another duration of that type.

Subtraction

You can subtract two date-times or two times to get a days and time duration. To subtract dates, you are supposed to use the *date and time* constructor function first, with time value midnight. But subtracting dates is very common, and I think this is a bug. You should be able to simply subtract dates to get a duration, and the Red Hat DMN runtime supports it. So this is what I recommend. You can also subtract two durations of the same type to get another duration.

Multiplication

You can multiply a duration times a number to get another duration of the same type, either days and time duration or years and months duration.

Division

You can divide a duration by another duration of the same type, returning a number. This is quite useful to convert a duration to a number. For example, to find the number of seconds in a year, use

```
duration("P365D")/ duration("PT1S")
```

Note that component extraction does *not* do this. The expression

```
duration("P365D").seconds
```

returns 0.

You can also divide a duration by a number to get another duration of the same type.

Example

Figure 154 is an example using calendar arithmetic. The customer is entitled to a refund if they return the purchase within a short interval. Decision *Refund Eligibility* has enumerated values "Full", "Partial", and "None". Input data *Return Timestamp* is a date-time. *Date of purchase* is a date.

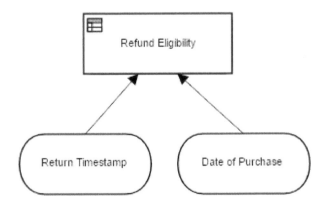

Figure 154. *Refund Eligibility* DRD

The customer gets a full refund if the return timestamp is less than 14 days from the date of purchase; partial refund if the timestamp is between 14 and 28 days inclusive from the date of purchase, and no refund if more than 28 days from date of purchase.

Refund Eligibility, a context, is shown in Figure 155. Context entry *DTduration* calculates the duration between return and purchase, and this value is used in the decision table *Eligibility*.

Refund Eligibility

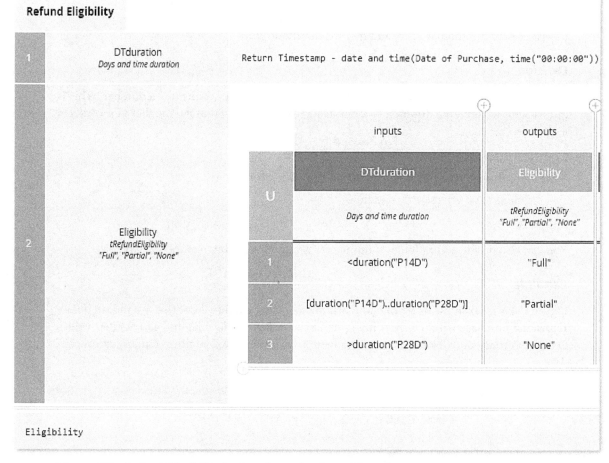

| 1 | DTduration *Days and time duration* | Return Timestamp - date and time(Date of Purchase, time("00:00:00")) |

| 2 | Eligibility *tRefundEligibility* "Full", "Partial", "None" | |

U	inputs	outputs
	DTduration *Days and time duration*	**Eligibility** *tRefundEligibility* "Full", "Partial", "None"
1	<duration("P14D")	"Full"
2	[duration("P14D")..duration("P28D")]	"Partial"
3	>duration("P28D")	"None"

Eligibility

Figure 155. *Refund Eligibility* logic using calendar arithmetic

CHAPTER 15

Handling Lists and Tables

One of the most powerful and useful features of DMN is its ability to handle lists and tables within its native expressions, so you don't need to exit to SQL, Java, or a process model for that.

What Is a List?

In DMN, a *list* is an ordered collection of values of the same type. Let's go through that piece by piece.

- *Ordered collection* means the list can contain multiple items – 0 or more – and the order of items in the list is significant. For example, the list [1,2,3] is not the same as the list [3,2,1]. If variable *A* is [1,2,3] and variable *B* is [3,2,1] then the expression *A=B* returns false. In FEEL, a comma-separated list of expressions enclosed in square brackets denotes a list.

- *Of the same type* means that if *a* is a string and *b* is a number, the list [*a,b*] is not valid. All items must be of the same type.

If the type of a list item is a structure, the list represents a *table*. For example, suppose the type *tLoan* has components *lender name, rate, points,* and *fee*. A list of items each of type *tLoan* thus defines a table of loans, one row per item in the list, and one column for each component of the structure. In DMN such a table is also called a *relation*. In this book, when I use the term *list* I mean both lists of simple values and tables. When I use the term *table*, I specifically mean a list of structured values.

Also, the type of a list item may itself be a list, defining a list of lists. A list of lists, like [[1,2], [3], [4,5]] is not the same as a table. In a table, each list item is a structure not a list.

DMN can do a lot with lists and tables. It can create or modify a list. It can test membership in a list, including various set operations. It can test whether any or all list items satisfy some condition. It can select items from a list and perform table lookups, queries, and joins. It can iterate some decision logic over each item in a list. And it can sort a list based on user-defined criteria.

Creating a List

DMN provides a multitude of ways to create a list. They include:

- List operator
- Decision table with Collect hit policy
- Value expression defined as a Relation
- List function
- Table component extraction
- Filter expression
- Iteration
- Recursion

List Datatypes

If an input data element, decision, or context entry is a list, it requires an item definition, or custom datatype, specifying it as a *collection*. In the Trisotech tool, if you want to say it is a list of text items, you need to define a new type, like *tStringList*, using the simple type *Text* and then click *Collection*. That puts the 3-bar collection icon in the datatype.

If the list item type is a structure, meaning the list is a table, we need two item definitions: one for an individual row, defining the components of the structure, and a second one defining a collection of that row type. For example, suppose we have *tLoanProduct* with the components *lenderName, rate, points,* and *fee*, and a second datatype *tLoanTable*, a collection of *tLoanProduct* items (Figure 156). While you could do it all in one type, putting the collection marker on *tLoanProduct*, I recommend using two types, since you often need to reference an individual row in the table, an individual loan product, and you need a type for that.

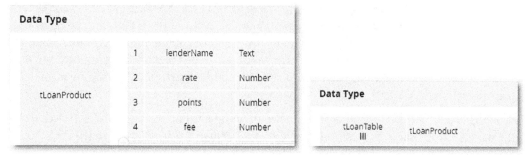

Figure 156. Tables have item definitions for both row and table types

List Operator

The simplest way to generate a list is a literal expression using the *list operator*, which is a pair of square brackets enclosing comma-separated items: [*item1, item2,* etc]. Remember, *item1, item2*, and all other members of the list must have the same datatype. The list operator is not limited to lists of simple values. If the list items are structures, then the list operator defines a table. For example, if the variables *Oceans*, *eClick1*, *eClick2*, and *AimLoan* are all of the same complex type *tLoanProduct*, then the list [*Oceans, eClick1, eClick2, AimLoan*] here creates the table shown in Figure 158.

Collect Decision Table

A *Collect decision table* also creates a list. Earlier in the book we saw hit policy C, for Collect, with an aggregation + for Sum, which adds together the number output values of all matching rules, generating a number. But C without aggregation generates a list, with one item per matching rule.

Collect decision tables are not frequently used, but here is an example. Suppose the variable *LoanProduct* is a structure with components *lenderName*, *rate*, *points*, and *fees*, and we want to generate from that *LoanAttributes*, a list of loan descriptors:

- If the *rate* is under 4%, we output the descriptor "Low rate"

- If *points* are zero, we output "No points"

- If *fees* are zero, we output "No fees"

- If both *points* and *fees* are zero, we output "no points or fees"

We could do it using a Collect decision table with four rules (Figure 157). Because more than one rule may match, the output is a list of *LoanAttributes*.

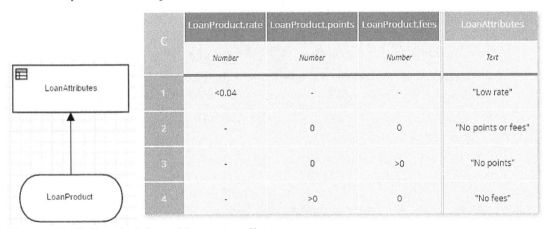

C		LoanProduct.rate	LoanProduct.points	LoanProduct.fees	LoanAttributes
		Number	Number	Number	Text
	1	<0.04	-	-	"Low rate"
	2	-	0	0	"No points or fees"
	3	-	0	>0	"No points"
	4	-	>0	0	"No fees"

Figure 157. Collect decision table creates a list

If no rules match, the output list is empty. This is allowed, and we represent an empty list as [].

Embedded Data Tables

You can embed data tables in your decision models using a decision with no information requirements, a so-called *zero-input decision*, defined as a *relation*. Figure 158 illustrates such a zero-input decision *Loan Table*, type *tLoanTable*. Zero-input relations such as this allow you to embed static data in the decision model without having to input it with each execution.

	lenderName	rate	points	fee
1	"Oceans Capital"	.03500	0	0
2	"eClick Lending"	.03200	1.1	2700
3	"eClickLending"	.03375	0.1	1200
4	"AimLoan"	.03000	1.1	3966

Figure 158. *Loan Table* **as a relation**

Generating a List from Another List

Actually, the most common way to generate a list in decision models is to manipulate another list. The original list may have come from a collection type input data, a list operator, Collect table, or relation, but most of the list variables you will use in DMN result from one of the following:

- A *list function* that takes a list as input and outputs a modified list. Examples include *append, concatenate, sublist, insert before,* and *sort.*

- A *filter expression* that selects a list of items from a starting list. Example: *LoanTable[pointsPct=0]* returns a list of *LoanTable* items.

- *Component extraction from a table* using the dot notation, returning a list of column values. Example: *LoanTable.lenderName* returns a list of lender names.

- *Iteration,* which applies some expression to each item in the original list to generate a list of output items. For example,

  ```
  for loan in LoanTable return Monthly Payment(loan)
  ```

  returns a list of payments.

We will talk about each of these in greater detail.

FEEL List Functions

Figure 159 shows the FEEL functions that operate on lists.

Function name	Result type	1st parameter	2nd parameter	3rd + parameter	
count	Number	list			count([1,2,3])=3
min, max	Item type	list			min([1,2,3])=1
min, max	Item type	c1	c2	c3...	max(1,2,3)=3
sum, mean	Number	list			sum([1,2,3])=6
sum, mean	Number	n1 (number)	n2 (number)	n3 (number)...	mean(1,2,3)=2
and, or (renamed all, any)	Boolean	list (of booleans)			Assume a=true, b=false all([a,b])=false; any([a,b])=true
and, or (renamed all, any)	Boolean	b1 (boolean)	b2 (boolean)	b3 (boolean)...	Assume a=true, b=false all(a,b)=false; any(a,b)=true
sublist	List	list	start position (number)	length? (number)	sublist([1,2,3],2)=[2,3] sublist([1,2,3],2,1)=2
append	List	list	item	item...	append([1,2,3],0)=[1,2,3,0]
concatenate	List	list	list	list...	concatenate([1,2,3],[0,1])=[1,2,3,0,1]
insert before	List	List	Number (start position)	Item	insert before([1,2,3],2,0)=[1,0,2,3]
list contains	Boolean	list	element		list contains([1,2,3],0)=false
remove	List	list	position (number)		remove([1,2,3],2)=[1,3]
reverse	List	list			reverse([1,2,3])=[3,2,1]
index of	Number list (of positions)	list	match		index of([1,2,3],3)=[3] index of([1,2,1,2,3],2)=[2,4]
union	List	list	list	list...	union([1,2,3],[1,2,4])=[1,2,3,4]
distinct values	List	List			distinct values([1,2,1,2,3])=[1,2,3]
flatten	List	list			flatten([[1,2],[2,3]])=[1,2,2,3]
product	number	list or $n_1...n_n$			product(2,3,4) = 24
median	number	list or $n_1...n_n$			median(8,2,5,3,4) = 4
stddev	number	list or $n_1...n_n$			stddev(2,4,7,5) = 2.0816659994661
mode	number	list or $n_1...n_n$			mode(6,3,9,6,6) = 6

Figure 159. FEEL built-in list functions

- *count* returns the number of items in the list.

- *min* and *max* select the minimum and maximum value of a list item, normally a number but possibly a date, time, or duration. And if a string, *min* and *max* are determined by alphabetical order. There are alternative syntaxes for *min* and *max*, either a single list argument, or a comma-separated list of items. The table shows both.

- *sum* and *mean* are similar, except they apply only to number items.

- The names of the DMN 1.1 functions *and* and *or* violate a DMN rule about function names conflicting with operator names, so they have been renamed *all* and *any* in DMN 1.2. These functions take either a single argument, a list of Boolean values, or multiple Boolean arguments. *all* returns true if all the arguments are true, and *any* returns true if any of the arguments are true.

- *sublist* extracts a portion of a list as another list. The second argument is the start position of the selection. If there is a third argument, it is the number of items extracted; if omitted, the function extracts all the items, starting from the position of the second argument. The examples in the table make it a little clearer.

- *append* and *concatenate* look similar, but they are not the same. *append* has a list argument and one or more item arguments. It creates a single list by appending the item arguments to the list argument. *concatenate* has one or more list arguments, and it combines them into a single list.

- *insert before* inserts a single item into a list at the position indicated by the second argument.

- *list contains* tests whether an item is contained in a list, true or false.

- *remove* deletes the item at a specific position from the original list.

- *reverse* generates a list with items in reverse order.

- *index of* outputs a list of positions where the list item value matches the test item value. The examples in the table illustrate this.

- *union* combines all items in multiple lists and removes duplicates.

- *distinct values* removes duplicates from a single list.

- *flatten* extracts all nested list items into a single flat list.

- *product, median, stddev,* and *mode* operate either on a number list variable or a sequence of number items, returning the product, median, standard deviation, and mode, respectively.

Filter Expressions

Filter expressions are one of the most useful features of FEEL. They are used to select items from a list or table. A filter expression is a list variable followed by an expression in square brackets, no commas. (In FEEL, square brackets could either mean a list generator or a filter expression, but you won't get them confused. If you have a list variable name followed immediately by square brackets, that's always a filter expression.)

The expression inside the square brackets, called the *predicate*, is either an *integer* or a *Boolean*. If it's an integer, it means select the item at that position in the list, always a single item. For example, *myList*[1] selects the first item in *myList*, *myList*[3] selects the third item. Negative numbers count from the end of the list: *myList*[-1] returns the last item in the list; *myList*[-2] returns the second to last.

A predicate that is a Boolean condition selects items from the list for which the condition is true. It is most often used to filter rows from a table. In a table, names referenced in the predicate represent columns of the table. For example,

```
Loan Table[rate<0.045]
```

selects a list of *Loan Table* rows for which the component *rate* is less than 0.045.

In a list of simple types, the keyword *item* means an item in the list. So *myList*[*item*>10] selects all items in *myList* with a value greater than 10. The syntax [table name].[component name] returns a list of column values corresponding to the named component. This syntax may also be used on a filtered table.

For example, Figure 160 is a relation defining *Loan Table 30*, an embedded table of loan products. The expression

```
Loan Table 30[rate<0.04].lenderName
```

filters the table to extract rows with a *rate* value less than 0.04, and from that extracts the *lenderName* value (Figure 161).

A filtered table may also be the argument of a list function. For example, the expression

```
count(Loan Table 30[pointsPct=0 and fees=0])
```

returns the count 5.

lenderName	rate	pointsPct	fees	term
Text	Number	Number	Number	Number
1 "AimLoan"	.0350	1.1	2637	360
2 "Amalgamated Bank"	.04000	0	1545	360
3 "AnnieMac"	.0375	0.1	442	360
4 "Aurora Financial"	.04125	0	0	360
5 "Bank of America"	.0400	0.465	1401	360
6 "Citibank"	.0425	0	2265	360
7 "Comerica"	.04190	0	104	360
8 "Commonwealth"	.03875	0	0	360
9 "Consumer Direct"	.03625	2	3636	360
10 "eLend"	.03990	0	0	360
11 "First Internet Bank"	.04000	0	0	360
12 "Home Point Financial"	.03875	0	0	360
13 "HomePlus"	.0425	0	842	360
14 "HSBC"	.04110	0	704	360

Figure 160. *Loan Table 30*, a relation

Low Rate Lenders

Loan Table 30[rate<0.04].lenderName

Figure 161. Filter query of *Loan Table 30*

A filter expression always returns a list. If no items satisfy the predicate expression, the result is the empty list [].

Special rules apply when the filter returns a *singleton list*, meaning a list with one item. This is quite common when the filter is selecting a table row using a primary key, such as an id field. In that case, the singleton list variable may be used without the predicate [1] to mean the list item in an expression that is not expecting a list.

For example, assume in *Loan Table 30* (Figure 160) that *lenderName* is a primary key. In that case, it is allowable to write

```
Loan Amount * Loan Table 30[lenderName = "AimLoan"].rate
```

instead of

```
Loan Amount * Loan Table 30[lenderName = "AimLoan"].rate[1]
```

even though technically this is a number multiplying a list of numbers, which is not normally allowed. The DMN 1.2 spec says the [1] may be omitted when the filter is known to extract a singleton list and the expression is expecting an item, not a list.

Iteration

A DMN expression can perform some decision logic repeatedly over each item in a list or each row in a table, and this is really useful. The iteration syntax uses the FEEL *for..in..return* operator:

```
for [range variable] in [list expression] return [output expression]
```

where *range variable* is a dummy name that means one item in the list defined by the *list expression*. The *output expression* is an expression – usually a function – involving the range variable and possibly additional arguments.

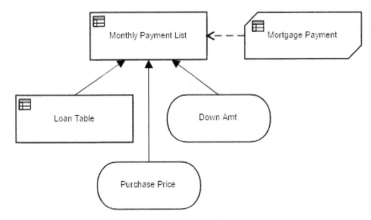

Figure 162. *Monthly Payment List* **DRD**

Figure 162 shows an example. The decision *Monthly Payment List* invokes the BKM *Mortgage Payment* once for each item in its input *Loan Table*. It uses the literal expression

```
for product in Loan Table return Mortgage Payment(product,
Purchase Price, Down Amt)
```

Here *product* is the range variable. There is no previously defined variable called *product*; it's just a dummy name that means *one row of Loan Table*.

Let's say the columns of *Loan Table* are *lenderName, rate, pointsPct, fee,* and *term*. The BKM *Mortgage Payment* returns the monthly payment for a single loan product, given the details of that product – *rate, pointsPct, fee,* and *term* – along with the purchase price and down payment amount (Figure 163). Here we see it is a context that calculates the *Loan Amount* from the *Purchase Price, Down Amt, pointsPct,* and *fees,* and then uses the amortization formula in the final result box. The decision *Monthly Payment List* iteratively invokes that BKM for each loan product in *Loan Table*. Since *Mortgage Payment* returns a number, the datatype of *Monthly Payment List* is a list of numbers, type *tNumberList*.

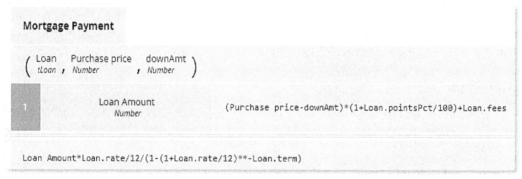

Figure 163. BKM *Mortgage Payment* calculates payment for a single loan product

The for..in..return syntax means take each row of *Loan Table*, invoke *Mortgage Payment* using arguments based on that row plus the input data *Purchase Price* and *Down Amt,* and collect the results in a list. The name we give the range variable doesn't matter. The only thing that matters about it is that we use the same name – *product*, here meaning a single loan product – in the BKM arguments.

Also note that it doesn't matter that the range variable name *product* does not match the BKM parameter name *Loan*. In the literal invocation syntax, it is the *order* of the arguments, not the parameter *names,* that matters. Here *Loan* is the first parameter, and *product* is the first argument in the invocation, so the value of *product* populates the parameter *Loan*.

Enhanced Iteration

This form of iteration iterates over *list item values*. It starts with a list expression and returns a list of equal length, one output item per item in the list expression. In DMN 1.2, iteration was enhanced with the ability to iterate over *list item positions* using the syntax

```
for [range variable] in [integer range] return [output expression]
```

where typically the output expression uses the range variable as an *index* to the list. The following example, a bit advanced, is from the *DMN Cookbook*.[27]

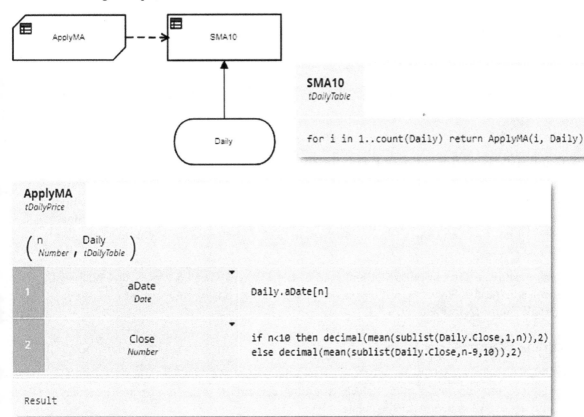

Figure 164. Simple moving average *SMA10* using enhanced iteration

Here input data *Daily* is a table of daily closing stock prices, with components *aDate* and *Close*. The BKM *ApplyMA* computes the 10-day simple moving average of the closing stock price on a certain date, that is, the mean of the closing price for that date and each of the 9 previous trading days. The decision *SMA10* returns the 10-day moving average for each date in *Daily* by iteratively invoking *ApplyMA*.

ApplyMA has two parameters: *n*, used as an index into the *Daily* table; and *Daily*, the table itself. It is modeled as a context with no final result box, meaning it creates a structure with one component per context entry. The component *aDate* selects the date column from *Daily*, using parameter *n* as an index:

```
Daily.aDate[n]
```

The component *Close* computes the 10-day moving average,

---

[27] https://www.amazon.com/dp/0982368186

```
decimal(mean(sublist(Daily.Close, n-9, 10)), 2)
```
which means:

- Extract the list of closing prices from daily.
- For the nth item in that list, select a sublist of 10 items starting with item number n-9.
- Take the mean of that sublist.
- Round the mean to 2 decimal places.

Note that the *Close* expression makes a minor adjustment for the first 9 items in the list, which do not have 9 previous items.

The enhanced iteration expression for *SMA10* is

```
for i in 1..count(Daily) return ApplyMA(i, Daily)
```

Here *i* is the range variable and the integer range is 1..count(*Daily*), using the same dotdot syntax we saw in decision table input entries, except here the range is understood to include integers only. Once again, the output expression uses the range variable as an argument. Since *ApplyMA* returns a structure with two components, *SMA10* returns a table with two columns, one row per date.

If this example is too complicated, don't worry. It's not something I'd expect most business modelers to tackle. However, if it makes complete sense to you, you may want to see similar examples in the *DMN Cookbook*.

Adding Columns to a Table

Putting aside the complexity of the enhanced iteration syntax, the previous example illustrates a very common use of iteration, which is adding columns to a table, or more generally, modifying the column structure of a table.

Here is how you do it.

First, you should have defined two datatypes for your original table, one for the row type and one for a collection of that type. Now you need to create two new types, one for a row in the new table with the column added, and a collection of that type.

Next, you need to define a BKM that maps one row of the original table to one row of the new table. One of the parameters of that BKM is a row of the original table; the others are whatever you need to add the new column. Model the BKM as a *context with no final result box*, one context entry per column of the new table.

Finally, iterate the invocation over the rows of the original table using for..in..return. The range variable provides the argument for the original row parameter in the BKM.

For example, the decision *Monthly Payment List* (Figure 162) is not in a particularly useful form. We'd prefer a table that shows the details of each associated loan product as well as the monthly payment, as shown in Figure 165. Here *Monthly Payment Table* is type *tLoan2Table*, a collection of type *tLoan2* (Figure 166). It is the same as the format for *Loan Table* with the addition of the column *payment*. We want our new column to be formatted as currency, so we'll use the *java format number* function discussed previously. That means the *payment* column type is going to be text, not number.

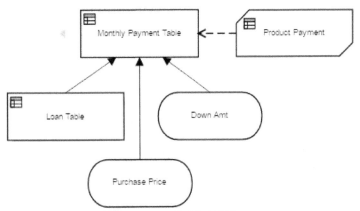

Figure 165. *Monthly Payment Table* **DRD**

tLoan2	1	lenderName	Text
	2	rate	Number
	3	pointsPct	Number
	4	fees	Number
	5	term	Number
	6	payment	Text

tLoan2Table	tLoan2

Figure 166. Item definitions for *Product Payment* **and** *Monthly Payment Table*

The BKM *Product Payment* (Figure 167) creates a single row of the *Monthly Payment Table*, taking a row of *Loan Table* and appending the formatted *payment* column. We use a context with no final result box, one context entry per column. The first BKM parameter, *product*, represents a row of *Loan Table*. The context entries for the original columns simply copy a component of *product* to the corresponding component of the new table. The new column, *payment*, is modeled as a nested context. It first calculates the *Loan Amount*. From that, it uses the amortization formula to calculate the *Monthly Payment*, a number. Then it invokes the previously discussed Java method to format *Monthly Payment* as currency with two digits following the decimal.

Monthly Payment Table (Figure 168) then iteratively invokes the BKM over each row of *Loan Table*. The result, using input data values *Purchase Price* 495000 and *Down Amt* 100000, is shown in Figure 169.

Product Payment

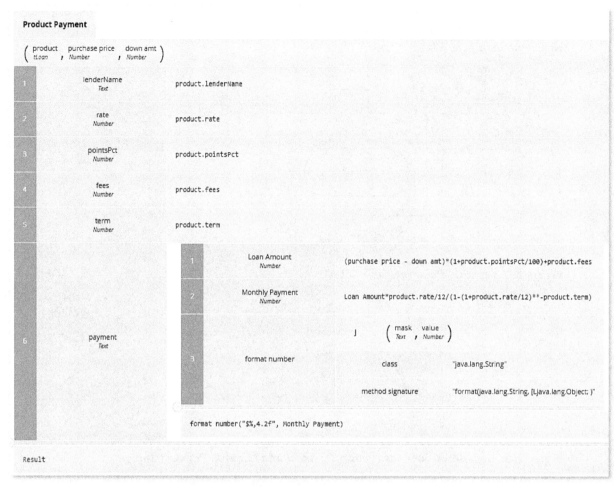

Figure 167. *Product Payment* creates one row of the table

Monthly Payment Table

```
for loan in Loan Table return Product Payment(loan, Purchase Price, Down Amt)
```

Figure 168. Iteration of *Product Payment* creates the table

lenderName	rate	pointsPct	fees	term	payment
Oceans Capital	0.035	0	0	360	$1,773.73
eClick Lending	0.032	1.1	2700	360	$1,738.71
eClickLending	0.03375	0.1	1200	360	$1,753.33
AimLoan	0.03	1.1	3966	360	$1,700.38
Home Loans Today	0.03125	1.1	285	360	$1,711.92
Sebonic	0.03125	0.1	4028	360	$1,711.03
AimLoan	0.03125	0.1	4317	360	$1,712.27
eRates Mortgage	0.03125	1.1	2518	360	$1,721.48
Home Loans Today	0.0325	0.1	822	360	$1,724.36
AimLoan	0.0325	0	1995	360	$1,727.75

Figure 169. *Monthly Payment Table* output

Testing All Members of a List

Iteration using for..in..return invokes a function – usually a BKM – once for each item in a list, and returns a list of the outputs of those invocations. There is a special case of iteration where the function being executed is a Boolean test, true or false, and the iteration returns not a list of true or false items but a single answer, true or false. The expression

```
some i in [list expression] satisfies [Boolean expression]
```

returns true if *any* item in the list satisfies the test, otherwise false. And the expression

```
every i in [list expression] satisfies [Boolean expression]
```

returns true if *every* item in the list satisfies the test, otherwise false.

Table Joins

Table joins are a familiar construct from database queries, where you want to select information from two separate tables linked by some common data element. FEEL supports table joins in various ways, including nested filter expressions, meaning a filter inside of another filter.

The general pattern is the expression

```
Table1[T1JoinColumn = Table2[innerFilter].T2JoinColumn].T1OutputColumn
```

The outer filter is the join, selecting rows of *Table 1* for which the join column value is equal to the join column value of the *Table 2* row selected by *innerFilter*, and then selecting the output column value for that row. That's assuming *innerFilter* returns a single row, which is not always the case.

Joins are a little tricky in FEEL because – as discussed previously – a filter always returns a list, even if it selects a single item. But recall that a singleton list acts like the item it contains in expressions that expect the item type, not a list type. In that case we can use comparison operators like = or > to compare a singleton list to an item. If the list contains multiple items, we must use the *list contains* function instead of equals in the join. This is easier to see with a couple examples.

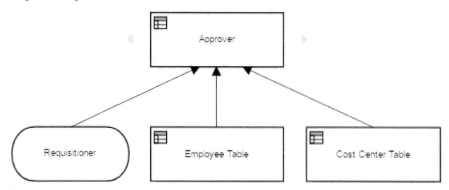

Figure 170. *Approver* DRD

Suppose we want to identify the *Approver* of an employee purchase requisition, which is specified as the manager of the employee's cost center (Figure 170). We have *Employee Table*, with columns *name, ID, cost center ID*, and *position*, and *Cost Center Table*, with columns *ID, name*, and *manager* (Figure 171). If we want to look up the manager of the employee named by the input data element *Requisitioner*, we join those tables using the *cost center ID*. The nested filter is

```
Cost Center Table[ID=Employee Table[name=Requisitioner].cost
center ID].manager
```

Let's break that down, working from the inside out.

```
Employee Table[name=Requisitioner].cost center ID
```

Employee Table

name	ID	Cost center ID	Position
Text	Text	Text	Text
"Anderson"	"A123"	"X45"	"Engineer"
"Baker"	"A136"	"Y2"	"Account Manager"
"Carson"	"A145"	"Y2"	"Receptionist"
"Davis"	"B755"	"Y2"	"Sales Consultant"
"Evans"	"A986"	"X46"	"Engineer"

Cost Center Table

ID	name	manager
Text	Text	Text
"Y1"	"Product Marketing"	"Smith"
"Y2"	"US Sales"	"Jones"
"Y3"	"EMEA Sales"	"Johnson"
"X45"	"Engineering"	"Kennedy"
"X46"	"Tech Support"	"Grant"

Figure 171. *Employee Table* **and** *Cost Center Table*

selects the row of *Employee Table* for the *Requisitioner* and then that individual's *cost center ID*, which is the field that links the two tables. The outer filter

```
Cost Center Table[ID=<the requisitioner's cost center ID>].manager
```

selects the row of *Cost Center Table* matching that *cost center ID*, and from that selects the *manager*. For example, if the *Requisitioner* is "Baker", the resulting *Approver* is "Jones".

In a second example, suppose we want to find the managers of all engineers. The *cost center ID* of all engineers is the filter

```
Employee Table[Position="Engineer"].cost center ID
```

Since engineers are in multiple cost centers, the filter returns a list with multiple IDs, not a singleton. In that case we can't use = to compare it to an *ID* from the *Cost Center Table*. Instead we must use the *list contains* function in the filter:

```
Cost Center Table[list contains(Employee
Table[Position="Engineer"].cost center ID, ID)].manager
```

The *list contains* function selects values of *Cost Center Table.ID* that are contained in the *cost center IDs* of engineers. And that is going to return a list of manager names, here "Kennedy" and "Grant".

List Membership and Set Operations

Item Membership

Testing whether some *individual item* is contained in a list occurs often in decision models, and DMN provides many ways to do it.

In a decision table, the item is a table input, and the list is the corresponding condition cell, the input entry, which should just contain the list name. It should not contain = or some other operator.

In a literal expression, DMN provides multiple alternatives:

- The *in* operator: *if [item] in [list expression] then…* For example, if the item is called *document type* and the list is *Critical documents*,

  ```
  if document type in Critical documents then...
  ```

- The *list contains* function. The first argument of this function is the list, the second is the item:

  ```
  if list contains(Critical documents, document type) then...
  ```

- Count of a filter:

  ```
  if count(critical document[item=document type])>0 then...
  ```

Set Operations

Testing whether *multiple items* are contained in a list is more complicated. The main reason is that in DMN a list is an *ordered sequence* of items. Also, the *in* operator and *list contains* function can test only membership of a single item in a list. Normally, determining if multiple items are contained in a list involves operations on *sets*, that is, unordered/deduplicated lists. And the membership test requires more specificity. For example, do you mean *is any item in list1 contained in list2?* Or, *are all items in list1 contained in list2?* Or, *which items in list1 are contained in list2?* You can do these *set operations* in FEEL literal expressions, but not in decision tables.[28]

I use the word *set* to mean an unordered deduplicated list. The FEEL functions *union* and *distinct values* remove duplicates but retain an ordering of the items. In fact, all lists in DMN are ordered, so you cannot define a variable as a set. But you can test whether *setA* intersects *setB*, i.e., has items in common, or whether *setA* is contained in *setB*, or whether *setA* is identical to *setB*. Here we mean that *setA* is the deduplicated unordered representation of *listA*.

Intersection

Let's start with *intersection*. The filter

---

[28] In DMN 1.2 it is possible to use the generalized unary test syntax to do it in a decision table, although not very business-friendly. For an example see the *DMN Cookbook*.

```
listA[list contains(listB, item)]
```

generates a list of items in *listA* that are also contained in *listB*. So it is an ordered version of the intersection of *setA* and *setB*, and may contain duplicates. We can remove duplicates with the *distinct values* function:

```
distinct values(listA[list contains(listB, item)])
```

We can apply the *count* function to this list to determine whether the sets intersect or not. A count of 0 means no intersection; a count greater than 0 means intersection. Alternatively, we can use the *some* operator, and this is actually more straightforward:

```
if some item in listA satisfies list contains(listB, item) then...
```

Containment

We can also test *containment:* Are *all* members of *setA* also members of *setB*? For this, use the *every* operator:

```
if every item in listA satisfies list contains(listB, item) then...
```

Identity

And finally, is *setA identical* to *setB*? We could test if both *setB* contains *setA* and *setA* contains *setB*, or we could use the *union* function, which concatenates *listA* and *listB* and then removes duplicates, in combination with the *every* operator:

```
if every i in union(listA, listB) satisfies (list contains(listA,
i) and list contains(listB, i)) then...
```

Sorting a List

DMN can sort a list or table using the FEEL *sort* function:

```
sort(list, precedes function)
```

The *sort* function is unusual because its second parameter is a *function definition* – not a value returned by a function invocation but the actual function definition. It took me a while to understand this. The second parameter of sort, called the *precedes function*, is a function that compares any two items in the list named by the first parameter and returns true if the first argument precedes the second argument in the sorted list.

There are two different ways to specify this precedes function. The more common way is to define it *inline*, that is, as an unnamed or "anonymous" function inside the parentheses of the sort invocation. An anonymous function definition uses the keyword *function* followed by parameters and a Boolean literal expression of those parameters. Here is an example.

Let's say *Loan Table* is a table of loan products and we want to sort it in ascending order of the loan *rate.* So it would look like this:

```
sort(Loan Table, function(x,y) x.rate<y.rate)
```

Loan Table is our list. An item in that list is a row in the table, a particular loan product. The parameters of the precedes function here are x and y, representing two arbitrary items in the list, two loan products in the table. The function definition says we will put product x ahead of product y in the sort if its *rate* value is less than y's *rate* value, in other words, *ascending order*. To sort in *descending* order of rates we would have *x.rate>y.rate*. To sort in *alphabetical* order of *lenderName*, we would have *x.lenderName<y.lenderName*.

When sorting tables, we often sort first by one column and then by a second column, when multiple items have the same value for the first column. And we can do that in FEEL as well:

```
if x.rate!=y.rate then x.rate<y.rate else x.pointsPct<y.pointsPct
```

In FEEL, != means not equal. In other words, sort by *rate*, but if two loan products have the same *rate*, sort those in ascending order of *pointsPct*.

Inline is the usual way to specify the precedes function, but you could create the precedes function definition independently of the sort function, as a BKM or a context entry, and then just specify its *name* as the second argument. The function definition must have two parameters with type matching items in the list to be sorted, and it must return a Boolean. Those are the only requirements. An independent sort function like this is used for more complicated sort logic. Again, readers interested in examples are referred to the *DMN Cookbook*.

Index

About the Author

Bruce Silver is Principal at Bruce Silver Associates, provider of consulting and training in business decision management and business process management. Through BPMessentials.com and methodandstyle.com, he is the leading provider of BPMN and DMN training and certification worldwide, with well over 4000 students trained using the Method and Style approach.

He is also a prolific author on process and decision modeling. His book *BPMN Method and Style 2nd edition*, with translations in German, Japanese, and Spanish, is considered the definitive standard on BPMN. His more recent *BPMN Quick and Easy* is a streamlined guide to process modeling aimed at business users. The first edition of *DMN Method and Style* introduced business users to the new decision modeling standard, and the second edition now updates the material to DMN 1.2. Finally, his book *DMN Cookbook*, written with Edson Tirelli, provides technical modelers and programmers solution, tricks, and workarounds using advanced FEEL and DMN boxed expressions.

He served on the BPMN 2.0 task force in OMG and currently serves on the DMN Revision Task Force. He was also a founder of the DMN TCK working group. In addition, he is founder and co-host of bpmNEXT, an annual conference showcasing the latest developments in business process and decision management technologies.

Prior to Bruce Silver Associates, he was Vice President and Service Director for workflow and document management at the analyst firm BIS Strategic Decisions, now part of Forrester Research. He has Bachelor and PhD degrees in Physics from Princeton and MIT, and holds four US Patents in electronic imaging. To contact him, email bruce@brsilver.com.

CPSIA information can be obtained
at www.ICGtesting.com
Printed in the USA
BVHW051613130920
588710BV00006B/232